STILL WATERS

AND

SKYSCRAPERS

THE 23RD PSALM
for the 21ST CENTURY

DAVE TOMLINSON

BakerBooks
Grand Rapids, Michigan

Published by Baker Books
a division of Baker Publishing Group
P.O. Box 6287, Grand Rapids, MI 49516-6287
www.bakerbooks.com

Printed in the United States of America

Library of Congress Cataloging-in-Publication Data
Tomlinson, Dave.
    Still waters and skyscrapers : the 23rd Psalm for the 21st century / Dave Tomlinson.
        p.   cm.
    Includes bibliographical references (p.   ).
    ISBN 10: 0-8010-6791-X (pbk.)
    ISBN 978-0-8010-6791-4 (pbk.)
    1. Bible. O.T. Psalms—Meditations. I. Title.
BS1430.54.T66 2006
242′.5—dc22   2006026863

First published in Great Britain in 2006

Society for Promoting Christian Knowledge
36 Causton Street
London SW1P 4ST

SPCK does not necessarily endorse the individual views contained in its publications.

STILL WATERS
AND
SKYSCRAPERS

Contents

Still Waters and Skyscrapers

I guess none of us can now look at a skyscraper without some consideration of 9/11, however faintly it may register in our consciousness. We received a psychic whack when the twin towers collapsed. The world could never be quite the same again. The skyscraper, a symbol of social and economic strength and prosperity, was transformed in a moment into an emblem of exposure and vulnerability. We live in a scary world. The tragedy of 9/11 was not the first event to convince us of this, yet the vision of those two mighty edifices falling to the ground in a heap of rubble rammed the message home with inexorable might.

Against the backdrop of such a terrifying event, and indeed, against the backdrop of untold scary developments in our world, Psalm 23 appears, on the face of things, archaic and irrelevant. Yet despite the quaintness of their speech and imagery, these fifteen lines of ancient Hebrew literature remain for millions of people the essential language of hope and trust in times of crisis, pain or loss. I am still haunted and moved by the thought of Todd Beamer, Oracle software executive and passenger on United's hijacked flight 93, reciting the Lord's Prayer and Psalm 23 with GTC switchboard operator Lisa Jefferson on his cell phone shortly before he perished with his fellow passengers and the terrorists.

So what is it about the pastoral imagery of a shepherd caring for his sheep that still inspires urbanites in New York, Los Angeles, London, Moscow and Paris? Why should people turn to this antiquated text for support and comfort in a world of concrete buildings, rush hour madness and international air travel? I suspect that Massachusetts rabbi Harold Kushner, goes to the heart of the issue when he says that the twenty-third psalm is the answer to the question: how do we live in a dangerous, unpredictable, frightening world?

Whether the crisis is a threat to national security or the devastating bereavement of a loved one, whether one faces the onset of illness or the loss of a job, whether one attends church regularly or hardly ever darkens its doors, reciting the familiar lines of Psalm 23 seems to act as a tranquilizer. For centuries, its ancient healing wisdom has guided people through dark and difficult circumstances.

Ironically, Psalm 23 offers no easy answers to hard questions, no shortcuts around life's nasty bits and no magic formula for solving life's problems. The writer is no starry-eyed religious romantic who imagines that life can be a breeze, a gentle saunter through lush meadows by babbling brooks. Yet still we find the psalm comforting and reassuring.

The twenty-third psalm offers what the Mennonite theologian Mary Schertz calls a "double consciousness"—a belief in the shepherd-God's providence, but a belief that in no way blinds the reader to the dark valleys that inevitably lie ahead.[1] The psalm evokes radical trust, not blind faith. The writer isn't offering some spiritual potion that can magically take away heartache, pain or loss; rather he is communicating what it means to trust in the midst of terror, grief, disappointment and frustration. He is telling us that there is meaning in situations where all our senses say that there is no meaning.

8

In London on July 7, 2005, four suicide bombers carried out coordinated bombings that killed fifty-two people and injured about seven hundred others. One of those killed was Jenny Nicholson, whose mother, Julie, is an Anglican priest. The agony of losing her lovely, vivacious twenty-four-year-old daughter has led Julie to step aside from parish ministry. She feels she cannot forgive Jenny's killers and cannot reconcile her role in presiding at the Eucharist with her unforgiveness. Julie Nicholson is passing through a very dark valley of grief. She still trusts in God, and she continues to exercise her priesthood in different ways. But she cannot pretend that all is well. The darkness is taking its toll.

I can't dare to speak for Julie, but I take heart from her integrity. She is grappling with the ambiguities of radical trust in the shepherd-God and honest acknowledgment of what she is experiencing on the inside.

Rabbi Kushner says that all his books—including the massive bestseller *Why Bad Things Happen to Good People*—have been inspired by the death of his fourteen-year-old son who was born with an incurable illness. Reflecting on Psalm 23, he concludes that the psalmist is not saying, "I will fear no evil because evil only happens to people who deserve it." He is saying, "This is a scary, out-of-control world, but it doesn't scare me, because I know that God is on my side, not on the side of the hijacker. God is on my side, not on the side of illness, or the accident or the terrible thing that happened. And that's enough to give me confidence."[2]

I shared Rabbi Kushner's thoughts with a woman in her mid-thirties who was raped last year. She has found it deeply healing to reframe her nightmare experience in the context of a shepherd-God who is on her side. Her memory of the event is being healed by the realization that she was not alone on that fateful night, even though she felt alone. She recites the twenty-third psalm regularly. She is finding her still waters. The world is still scary. But not so scary as it once was.

INTRODUCTION

WHY READ THE PSALMS?

When police officers are going through their training, one of the exercises they must perform is to give a running commentary as they are driving. This involves making verbal observations on everything that's happening, on and around the road—commenting on the conditions, any other cars that are around, pedestrians, and so on. They call it "talking your way through" the situation.

When my brother was training to be a police officer in Liverpool, he would come home with all kinds of horror stories, some of which were doubtless apocryphal, but entertaining all the same. One time he told us about a trainee who was driving a fast car in the Lake District accompanied by three instructors. As the driver turned a bend he was faced with a very long and gradual hill. Halfway up the hill was a slow-moving car. And at the brow of the hill a very large truck was just appearing, coming in the opposite direction. The police car was traveling at about 80 mph at this point. Then to the trainee's deep dismay, one of the instructors coolly said, "Put your foot hard down and talk your way through it." Filled with terror and struggling to take in the directive, which he knew he must obey, the young trainee pulled out to face the oncoming truck, shoved his foot hard on the gas and in a shaky voice said, "The Lord is my shepherd, I shall not want. . . ."

If there is one chapter in the Bible that countless people in the English-speaking world—including this police officer—could have a crack at reciting by heart, it is the twenty-third psalm. And even if they couldn't reel it off perfectly, many would be able to mumble their way through it with others in a congregation. The psalm probably had particular resonance with the police officer, since it is best known as the funeral psalm. Indeed, I can reliably inform you that Psalm 23, set to the familiar tune Crimond, is still the number one hit on the funeral charts. And the reason is pretty straightforward: it's a very calming, reassuring psalm.

And yet for many of us who have grown up with Psalm 23, it is easy to treat it as little more than a religious cliché, a sappy piece of verse generally accompanied by images of tranquil lakes and meadows, and a bearded shepherd caressing little lambs—often with a sickly smile on his face. It's a picture well suited to Sunday school classrooms and old people's homes. But what, if anything, does the "shepherd's psalm" have to say to us urbanites, more familiar with concrete buildings, rush hour traffic and police sirens than with green pastures, calm lakes and shepherd's crooks?

And yet Psalm 23 does still work—it's an icon of peace and security in troubled times. But it is essentially at a symbolic level that it tends to work. Not too many mourners at a graveside contemplate the meaning of the psalm or dissect it stanza by stanza. Yet I believe the content is very powerful; there is a wisdom and spirituality about this psalm that can only be perceived through meditation. So in this book I'm going to be unpacking the wisdom and spirituality of the twenty-third psalm. But first, by way of introduction, I want to make some observations about the

Psalms in general, so that we can get a better grip on the language and context of Psalm 23.

There is another psalm that has gained some popularity in recent years among a certain section of the population, namely U2 fans—Psalm 40. Those of you who have attended U2 gigs over the years will know that for a long time the band always finished the show with "40."

In show after show, hundreds of thousands of fans "of every size and shape t-shirt," as Bono puts it, have shouted back the refrain (pinched from Psalm 6): "How long, to sing this song." I wonder how many of them realized that they were singing an ancient prayer to God!

Clearly, Bono finds the Psalms fascinating. A few years ago he contributed a prologue to the Book of Psalms for the Pocket Canon series, which gave all kinds of famous people the opportunity to write an introduction to their chosen book from the Bible. Psalms and hymns, Bono tells us, were his first taste of inspirational music. He says that words and music did for him what solid, even rigorous, religious argument could never do: they introduced him to God, not belief in God, but more an experiential sense of God. "My religion could not be fiction," he writes, "but it had to transcend facts."

Now that takes us to a very important feature of the Psalms: they are art, and they are poetry. They grapple with truth at a different level than propositions and so-called "facts." Their language is not the language of logic or reasoned argument, but the language of feelings and imagination. The Psalms are the guts of the Bible. The writers make no attempt to be religiously or ethically correct; they pour out their emotions and reactions in honest, gutsy encounters with the Almighty.

Anyone who reads the Psalms systematically, rather than simply dipping into the old favorites, soon discovers that they aren't all as calming, reassuring and comforting as Psalm 23. Some are dance numbers (literally), others are blues songs, some are pretty disturbing in their tone and a few are downright obnoxious!

Psalm 137, for example, opens with the line immortalized by Boney M: "By the rivers of Babylon; there we sat down, and we wept when we remembered Zion." But don't let the catchy tune and the dance rhythm deceive you: Psalm 137 is a moody lament from an angry soul who has been abducted and forced to live in a foreign land. He's thoroughly fed up. And it gets worse. As he looks on his oppressors, his anger boils: "Happy shall they be who take your little ones and dash them against the rock!" You can see why Boney M left out that bit.

But hang on. It wasn't us who were taken hostage; it wasn't our children who were slaughtered by an invading force; it wasn't our homes and belongings that were looted and burned; it wasn't our dreams that were shattered. Is this how the parents of the Moors murder victims feel? My liberal (and I hope Christian) sentiments inclined me to see Myra Hindley released before she died—but it wasn't my precious kids who were snatched away and brutally murdered, their fragile bodies buried in shallow graves out there on the cold, lonely moors of Saddleworth.

The Psalms do not simply offer happy-clappy, sanitized religion; they voice ecstatic joy, passion, disappointment, pain and grief. This is gut-level religion, a spirituality acquainted with the dark sides of life as well as the seasons of "sweetness and light." The Book of Psalms expresses honest, gut-level, straight from the hip human experience passing through the varied seasons of life.

I marvel at how the religious censors of the past managed to keep their scissors away from some of the Psalms. Perhaps they recognized the necessity of powerful, unedited conversations with God in Holy Scripture if real honesty was to be preserved in the reader's spirituality. Here we have authentic humanity—sometimes rapturously applauding the Almighty, other times groping for him through darkness, pain and despair, and sometimes hounding heaven for justice, or even revenge—the full gamut of creaturely emotions. Oh yes, this is gut-level religion all right.

And if the Psalms tell us anything, they tell us that life runs in seasons. You may be experiencing such warm sunshine that you despise the miserable person who drones on with endless soul-searching. But beware: you may soon be gazing into a Babylonian river yourself, longing for things to be different and ready to bash the blasted happy-clappy chorus-singer over the head with his own guitar!

Walter Brueggemann, in *The Message of the Psalms*, offers three categories into which most of the Psalms fit. The first category is what he calls psalms of *orientation*. These psalms reflect a state of settledness or normality—all is well, things are as they should be, God is in the heavens, peace prevails on earth. Then Brueggemann talks about psalms of *disorientation*. These are the psalms that express a sense of disturbance or dislocation—all is not well, things are going wrong, life feels disordered. These are the psalms of lament, pain and protest. Third, there are psalms of *new orientation*, psalms that begin to contain a sense of disturbance and disorientation, but then incorporate a surprise turn of events: God intervenes, hope enters the picture and there is a sense of resolve. Brueggemann puts Psalm 23 in this category for reasons we'll come to later.

In the context of the New Testament, we can say that the disciples' experience of being with Jesus throughout his ministry was their time of orientation or normality—which they desperately wanted to hang on to forever. The crucifixion signaled a shift to disorientation—everything that could go wrong did go wrong. But the resurrection was a season of new orientation, of incredible surprise.

So within the entire spectrum of the Psalms, all aspects of human experience are represented. What's more important, they are all placed in the context of a gut-level conversation with God. And yet, the fact is, you could spend your entire life in many churches and never know that it is normal to experience dry times in your spiritual life, sad times, downright fed-up times and ready to strangle the next person who says "Praise the Lord" times! And the thought that you might acceptably express anger or disappointment with the divine never enters the minds of lots of Christians. Yet it's essential that we learn to do so.

I have found that the Christians who go on the most about the authority of Scripture and believing the Bible from cover to cover generally belong to churches that read the Bible selectively, and they love to sing and quote all the nice bits of the Psalms with hardly a mention of the unpleasant bits.

So thank God for the Book of Psalms: the charter of gut-level religion, a spirituality for all seasons. We can't identify with all of the sentiments all of the time, but seasons change. And if you can't pray a particular psalm for yourself now, pray it for someone else. The Psalms are the prayer of the mystical body of Christ *par excellence*, because when we pray them we are crying out not only in our own name but in the name of all humanity.

The Psalms are about authentic humanity and authentic religion. They call us to levels of honesty within ourselves and toward God that are not always comfortable to live with. But the only way I can truly meet God is, as the old hymn says, "just as I am." That's the Book of Psalms. That's reality. That's gut-level religion.

"THE LORD IS MY SHEPHERD"

Is anybody out there?

During the autumn of last year I was called to the deathbed of a lovely old lady in the parish. She had been bedridden for some years and had been cared for by her son until his untimely death six months earlier. She never recovered from his passing. No parent expects to bury his or her child, but to lose the son who was with her and who cared for her seven days a week was simply too much to bear. I had officiated at his funeral, and now I sat at her bedside, knowing that soon I would be officiating at hers.

The woman's family was distressed by her constant agitation. "If only Mom could relax and just let go," her daughter said. Not knowing how much the dying woman could hear or understand, I gently took her hand and read the King James Version of the twenty-third psalm: "The Lord is my shepherd, I shall not want. . . ." As I came to verse 4, "Yea, though I walk through the valley of the shadow of death, I will fear no evil: for thou art with me," I felt her squeeze my hand firmly. Then, as I finished the psalm, she relaxed, the tension melting from her face. Within a few hours she was gone, her soul resting peacefully in the arms of the Great Shepherd.

The effectiveness of Psalm 23 is not rooted in some rational understanding of what it says. A woman on her deathbed, or a group of mourners around a grave, do not pause to contemplate the meaning of each stanza in the psalm; its capacity to breathe comfort and confidence to those facing life's hardest moments works at a much more symbolic level. There are two factors here. First, the psalm is deeply embedded in the culture and psyche of the English-speaking world; hearing the familiar tones of the King James Version of Psalm 23 evokes a collective memory, a sense of hope in times of crisis. Second, the psalm hinges on the simple yet compelling imagery of a shepherd watching over his flock. Psalm 23 is a shining example of the way in which a metaphor or picture brings to life a fundamental affirmation of faith—"God is love"—and infuses it with emotional energy. Without the image of a shepherd-God, our grasp on the nature of the divine may be quite different.

"The Lord is my shepherd." To utter these words is to affirm trust that within and beyond our scary world there exists a loving, benevolent presence—someone who cares about us. Our tiny, insignificant lives matter. But how does that belief translate into any kind of reality when we are facing death or dealing with the loss of a loved one? Or indeed, in situations like the bombings that took place in London in July 2005?

Psalm 23 does not offer the hope of constant happy endings or the suggestion that bad things will not happen to good people. Indeed, the psalm centers on the reality of death and the dark shadow it casts over our lives, and on the recognition that enemies—those who seek our harm—do exist. The psalm takes us, in fact, on a journey: from an initial sense of calm in the opening verses, through a dark valley of grief in the middle verses, into a place of renewed serenity in the house of the Lord at the end. Psalm 23 does not say that bad things will not happen; what it says is that we do not have to face them on our own—"for thou art with me."

In *The Lord Is My Shepherd*, Rabbi Harold Kushner writes that "religion is our human response to the dual reality of being alive and knowing that we have to die." The one great fear we share is that of ultimately being alone. One man, describing the horror of a pitch-black carriage on the London Underground after one of the bombs exploded, said that people were praying aloud and calling out to God. Those of us who did not pass through the dark valley of London's devastation cannot begin to imagine how dark it was. Yet some part of the shadow of these events was cast on us all. One of the most moving elements of a situation like this is the driving passion felt by everyone to get home. One man was quoted as saying that it would take him until midnight to walk home, but nothing would stop him from making the six-hour journey. The one thing we fear is to be left alone.

The message of Psalm 23 is that we are never alone, that our lives are not meaningless, that someone cares about what happens to us. Unlike many of the Psalms, the twenty-third is deeply personal. It is about an individual's relationship with God: "The Lord is *my* shepherd" (italics added). Jesus, speaking as the Good Shepherd, says, "I know my own sheep and my own know me." Some will say, "Ah, there you are. It's a holy club, and if you're not a member you've had it." People often say to me: "He never went to church, is that all right? Can you still bury him and say prayers for him?" Jesus shattered the club mentality: "I have other sheep that do not belong to this fold," he said. "I must bring them also, and they will listen to my voice. So there will be one flock, one shepherd." Time and again I say to people, "God loves you no less because you don't go to church, or because you've lost your way or made a mess of things or because you can't bring yourself to believe."

The love of the shepherd-God for his sheep is unconditional. There are no "ifs" or "buts" about God's love for us: "*If* you go to church"; "*If* you put lots of money in the collection"; "*If* you are clever enough to understand com-plicated theological questions"; "*If* you are successful, or popular or good-looking"; "*If* you have a nice little tidy life, a husband or wife and 2.3 children"; "*If* you are a white Anglo-Saxon, a Christian rather than a Jew or a Muslim, a heterosexual rather than a gay, and so on." God loved us before we were born, and he will love us through death and beyond. As Henri Nouwen says in *Bread for the Journey*, "God's love is from eternity to eternity and is not bound by any time-related events or circumstances." Does this mean that what we do or don't do is of no consequence? Of course not. Unconditional love is not the same as unconditional approval. Parents may love their children whatever they do, but this doesn't stop them from grieving about the hurt their offspring inflict on themselves and others.

It's been said that the twenty-third psalm is an earlier form of the parable of the prodigal son. The psalmist finds himself in a dark and barren place, in the presence of en-emies, a long way from home, but eventually he returns to his father's house. More of that later; it is sufficient for now to say that the real point of both this parable and Psalm 23 is that we can never wander beyond the reach of God's loving presence. A soldier perishing on a desolate battlefield, a drug addict overdosing in an empty room, a rush-hour commuter dying in the darkness of a bombed-out tube train—God is there; no one is truly alone: "The Lord is my shepherd."

Inevitably, this leads us back to the well-worn question: why doesn't God do something to stop acts of evil, bru-tality and injustice in our world? Why doesn't the Good Shepherd do a better job of protecting his sheep? Rabbi Harold Kushner responds to the question by pointing to the great Christian image of the *Pieta*, a sculpture created by Michelangelo in 1498. The *Pieta* shows Mary holding the broken body of her son on her lap, looking at him with such tenderness and sorrow that, as the rabbi says, one

21

doesn't have to share Christian belief in the theological significance of the crucifixion to be moved by the image. The only problem, he says, is that it portrays a scene that probably did not take place: there is no indication in the Bible that Mary held Jesus when he was taken down from the cross.

So how can Michelangelo's *Pieta* move us so deeply, Kushner asks, if it didn't take place? The significance, he suggests, is not in the literalness of what is portrayed, but in what it symbolizes. The woman in the sculpture holding the broken body of Jesus is not Mary, Kushner ventures, but God: God in feminine form, a God "who grieves for his children when they suffer, who suffers with them when they are cruel to one another, when they hurt and kill one another." Everyone who suffers the loss of a loved one is reenacting God's grief at the death of any one of his children. Kushner quotes the Reverend William Sloane Coffin, the radical peace activist, who commented after the death of his own son, "God's was the first heart to break." Psalm 23 offers no promise of a safe passage through life; rather it assures us that we are not alone when we pass through the valleys of pain, suffering and loss.

Whenever we see illustrations of Psalm 23, they usually show a bearded shepherd with an insipid smile, holding a lamb in his arms. The reality of life for the ancient shepherd was harsh. He couldn't take off at 5 p.m. and go home for dinner, then return to the flock at 9 a.m. the following day. Shepherds lived with their sheep 24/7. The relationship was intimate: the shepherd knew each of his sheep individually; he cared for them when they were sick, risked his life to protect them from wild animals and constantly led them to new pastures and ample water supplies. The shepherd was with the sheep all the time. "The Lord is my shepherd."

It is interesting that the most common pictorial representation of Christ in early Christian art—consistently chosen in preference to images of crucifixion or kingship—is that of the Good Shepherd. And it has a particular influence on the iconography of baptisteries that can be traced from the painting of the Good Shepherd beside the font of a third-century Syrian house-church to the stained glass in Victorian churches. When we baptize our children we entrust them to the abiding presence and care of the shepherd-God. When adults are baptized they set out on a journey, committed to following the shepherd of their souls.

Christianity does not offer straightforward, neat answers to life's hard questions. Faith does not hinge on a totally rational philosophical framework. Despite our best efforts to grapple with the mysteries of human existence, we are left with as many questions as answers. Faith is not about certainty, but about trust. We trust that, despite the evil of pointless atrocities, there is a purpose to life, to history, to personal existence. We trust in a divine benevolence at the heart of the cosmos: that love will overcome hatred, goodness will outlive evil, wisdom will prevail over stupidity, justice will outlast prejudice and discrimination, poverty will be history and kindness will triumph over self-interest. Above all, we hope. And what greater symbol of hope can there be than a child welcomed into the flock of God?

The world is a scary place. Acts of terrorism make it seem even scarier. But we have a choice. We can withdraw and seek safety in isolation and submit to the fear and terror of what may be, or we can draw strength from the presence of the shepherd-God and go out into that scary world. We can commit to creating an atmosphere of courage, trust and serenity, out of which the adventure of a new world order will emerge. Leaders from eight major countries of the world's economy gather in an annual meeting called the G8 summit to discuss topics of mutual or global concern. During the 2005 G8 summit, we saw people of all faiths and no faith united in a resolve to create a more just and equitable world, a world where kindness and mutual consideration is much more than a mere sentiment.

When we recite the twenty-third psalm in times of trouble or uncertainty, we invoke within ourselves trust in the Good Shepherd. And the central affirmation of the psalm is that "thou art with me." God does not promise an easy ride, a safe passage, a trouble-free life; he promises to be with us, the Great Shepherd of our souls. I invite you to affirm your own trust in the Lord, your shepherd. I invite you to say three times: thou art with me.

> Thou art with me.
> Thou art with me.
> Thou art with me.

"I SHALL NOT WANT"

WHAT WE REALLY, REALLY WANT

Have you come across the website www.iwantoneofthose
.com, the site that offers "stuff you don't need . . . but you
really, really want"? The current top ten products offered
include an inflatable Sumo Wrestler Suit that enables you to
appear hundreds of pounds heavier for a mere seventy-five
dollars. Then there's the Aurora Mood Clock that changes
color every hour on the hour to treat you to the benefits
of chromotherapy (color therapy). And there's the Bath
Caddy, "one of life's little heavens": a frame that goes across
the bath with a book stand, two wineglass holders and a
candle holder. The whole thing is constructed, we are told,
from polished metal, with the handles coated in soft white
rubber to prevent scratching!

What do you want? What do you really, really want?
Psalm 23 says, "The Lord is my shepherd, I *shall not* want"
(italics added). That's a huge statement. What does it mean?
Surely we all want things. We may not be looking for a chromotherapy clock or a sumo wrestler suit, but we do want
things: somewhere to live, a decent job, good health for
ourselves and our loved ones, happiness for our children,
peace of mind, no more suicide bombings in London or
anywhere else. So what does it mean: "I shall not want"?

The first thing to say is that in the original text, "I shall not want" does not mean "all my desires can be realized." A better translation is, "I shall lack for nothing." This isn't a blank check for whatever we fancy, but a statement of deep trust: "The Lord is my shepherd: I know everything will be okay. I know someone is looking out for me."

There are two very broad ways of looking at life. The first is to assume that there is no God; that human beings are fundamentally alone in the cosmos. According to this way of seeing things, human life is essentially random, a chance occurrence; there is no bigger plan into which our existence fits, no greater purpose behind the events of our lives, no ultimate framework in which to interpret them. If this is how things are, it is very easy to arrive at the conclusion that looking after number one is what really matters: we get what we can from life, try to control our own destiny and replace altruistic ideals with hard-nosed reality.

The alternative perspective is to believe that there is purpose and meaning to life, that a loving presence pervades our otherwise futile existence, drawing us (if we will be drawn) ever closer to the fulfillment of our creaturely destiny. Psalm 23 affirms this way of seeing things. The assertion, "The Lord is my shepherd, I shall not want," is an expression of belief in a greater reality than the day-to-day reality of pain, suffering and death, of bombs, hunger and injustice. It's saying, "I believe in something more."

"The Lord is my shepherd, I shall not want," is not saying, "God is on my side, I shall have whatever I want." Nor is it saying, "I am never going to experience hurt or disappointment or failure because God won't let these things happen to me." Instead, it insists that, come what may, God will always be with us—and that this will prove to be more than enough.

Jesus makes the point that God sends rain on the righteous and on the unrighteous; both believers and unbelievers go on wanting plenty of things throughout their lives.

What we pray for so seldom seems to be clearly given. Yet as Frederick Buechner points out in *The Clown in the Belfry*, perhaps when the psalm says, "I shall not want," it is in fact speaking the ultimate and absolute truth:

> Maybe it means that if we keep our eyes open, if we keep our hearts and lives open, we will at least never be in want of the one thing we want more than anything else. Maybe it means that whatever else is withheld, the shepherd never withholds himself, and he is what we want more than anything else.

The one thing we all desire is to not feel alone. Two very hopeful stories illustrate this. Elisabeth Kübler-Ross, a psychiatrist who specialized in helping people deal with death, told in *On Children and Death* the story of a little boy with whom she once worked who was in the final stages of leukemia. She asked him to draw a picture that showed her how he was feeling about his illness. He drew a dark and scary self-portrait with thunderclouds in the sky and a cannon pointed directly at his heart. When Kübler-Ross saw it, she did not say anything or try to change his feelings. Instead, she quietly took the picture and added something to it. She sketched a figure of herself in a white coat, standing close to the little boy in the picture, facing the cannon with him, her arms securely around his shoulders. A few days later, her young patient drew another picture. In this one the sun was shining, there were flowers everywhere and he had a huge smile on his face. He no longer felt alone.

The other story is about a now famous picture of premature twin girls, born in 1995. In accordance with hospital policy, each child was placed in a separate incubator, but one was very weak and not expected to survive. Their primary nurse fought against hospital rules and decided to place both babies in one incubator. When they were put together, the healthier of the two threw an arm over her sister in what looks like an endearing embrace. As a result, the smaller baby's heart rate stabilized and her temperature rose to normal. Both babies survived, and eventually went home where they continued to share a crib. After seeing the effect of putting the two girls together, the hospital changed its policy and allowed multiple-birth babies to be placed in the same incubator.

If only we can but discern his presence, the shepherd-God is always with us. Often that presence is experienced through the warmth and companionship of other people: the loving care of a friend or relative, the compassion of a healthcare professional, even the unconscious hug of a teeny sibling in an incubator. Other times it is experienced through the wonder of the world around us or through a deep inner peace that makes no sense in the situation; sometimes we know it in the hurly-burly of everyday life, other times in a quiet moment when we manage to escape the demands of the daily routine. The healing wisdom of the twenty-third psalm is that the shepherd-God is always with us. And to utter the words, "The Lord is my shepherd, I shall not want," is to place ourselves, consciously, into the matrix of God's love.

The rest of Psalm 23 is basically an interpretation of the statement, "I shall not want." In other words, it's a description of what life is like for those who put their trust in the Lord. As we have already seen, a life of trust is not a life free from failure, pain or loss, but a life of peace and confidence even in confusing and frightening times.

But there's more to it than that. To say with faith, "I shall not want," is also to make a decision that in the face of the greed, lust, overindulgence and competitiveness of a consumerist culture, we embrace a spirit of "enoughness." As Walter Brueggemann observes in *The Threat of Life*, "Our consumer society is driven by the notion that we always must want one more thing, and we are entitled to it, and we will have it no matter what." "I shall not want" is therefore a countercultural statement, a vision of contentment in a culture of "I want."

The twenty-third psalm is a long way, I think, from the televangelists' so-called "prosperity gospel"—a doctrine that insists that if we have enough faith (and make generous donations to the particular preacher's organization) our finances will flourish and we will be successful in business, enjoy blissful relationships and experience physical and spiritual health. This is simply the "I want" culture dressed up in misconstrued Bible verses and theological hogwash.

The spirituality of the twenty-third psalm is a spirituality of contentment. Instead of saying, "Please God, give me what I want," we say, "I lack nothing. I already have what truly matters: I know I will never face life alone." To arrive at this point is to have refocused our desires, to realize that most of our wants are contrived and imagined and phony. I say again, Psalm 23 makes no promise of material, emotional or physical prosperity; what it offers is peace of mind even in the darkest times.

The spirituality of the twenty-third psalm is also a spirituality of gratitude: it tends to invoke prayers that begin with "Thank you . . ." rather than "Please give me . . ." Walking around a record store recently, I was brought to a halt as the words of a Dido song filled the air: "Well I deserve nothing more than I get, 'cause nothing I have is truly mine." Resisting the temptation to shout out "Amen," I pondered Dido's line all the way home, feeling ever more grateful for the untold mercies I experience day by day, and humbly accepting that each of them is a gift and not a right.

It's for this reason that, speaking as a Christian rather than a Jew, I see Psalm 23 as a eucharistic hymn. Later on the psalm speaks about a table being set and a cup running over: images that immediately evoke in Christians thoughts of the Eucharist. The word *Eucharist* means "thankfulness." To partake of the holy mysteries, as to utter the words of the twenty-third psalm, is to acknowledge beyond doubt that salvation, like life itself, is a gift.

Yet, in reality, it is hard to understand why things we want, let alone things we feel we need, are sometimes taken away. How tempting it is in these troubled times to conclude that life is indeed random, that there is no pattern or higher purpose to things. As Madeleine L'Engle puts it in *Glimpses of Grace*: "There are many times when the idea that there is indeed a pattern seems absurd wishful thinking. Random events abound. There is much in life that seems meaningless." Yet she goes on to say, "And then, when I can see no evidence of meaning, some glimpse is given which reveals the strange weaving of purposefulness and beauty."

The spirituality of Psalm 23 offers no black and white explanations; the questions persist. Yet beyond the questions, beyond the doubts and ambiguities, this psalm breathes confidence: the palpable sense that there is always more to life than we can grasp or understand. And yet we keep on looking, searching, inquiring, adventuring with the Almighty—keeping holy discontent alive too. So perhaps there is a legitimate sense in which we must keep on wanting: wanting in the sense of exploring, dreaming, delving, longing and yearning.

Rabbi Harold Kushner sums it all up rather well in his alternative version of the opening verse of the psalm:

> The Lord is my shepherd; I shall often want. I shall yearn, I shall long, I shall aspire. I shall continue to miss the people and the abilities that are taken from my life as loved ones die and skills diminish. I shall probe the empty spaces in my life like a tongue probing a missing tooth. But I will never feel deprived or diminished if I don't get what I yearn for, because I know how blessed I am by what I have.

"He makes me lie down in green pastures"

FOOD FOR THE SOUL

"He makes me lie down in green pastures" is the psalmist's way of saying that the shepherd-God will satisfy our deepest needs, our deepest hungers. The picture painted in Psalm 23 is of well-tended, well-fed sheep, grazing in verdant pastures and drinking from clear, calm waters. It's a scene of plenitude and abundance. These are sheep that want for nothing.

In many ways, we experience a great deal of abundance, simply by living in the Western world, where we hardly know what scarcity or shortages mean. Yet in his challenging book *Culture Jam: The Uncooling of America*, Kalle Lasn warns that while most of us tend to associate suffering with material deprivation, plenitude or overabundance also results in suffering of a different kind. There is a "perverse burden" carried by people who have everything they could possibly want and yet who still don't think it is anywhere near enough. "When everything is at hand," he says, "nothing is ever hard-won, nothing ever satisfies. Without satisfaction, our lives become shallow and meaningless . . . we embrace the value of More to compensate for lives that seem somehow, Less. . . . Plenitude feeds malaise as it fills the stomach."

I was thinking about Lasn's comments recently when I watched two back-to-back TV news items. The first reported on the famine in Niger that threatens the lives of 3.6 million people, including 800,000 children. The other described the United Kingdom's growing problem of adult and child obesity. Poverty and starvation in countries like Niger certainly pose a more acute problem than anything we experience in the West, yet perhaps obesity, with all its attendant health risks, is symbolic of the "perverse burden" created by plenitude that Lasn talks about.

But the West is not simply overfed, it is also vastly overstimulated. I recently read that a single edition of the *Times* contains more information than the average person in Tudor England processed in an entire lifetime. Assuming that is true, imagine how many Shakespearean lifetimes of information bombard us every week from television, radio, newspapers, books, magazines and, most of all, the Internet. A mere click of a computer mouse unleashes a tidal wave of words, images and information.

In the interest of integrity, I should probably admit to being a pretty serious techno junkie myself. We have broadband wirelessly transmitted throughout our house; I use the Internet on a daily basis; my wife, Pat, complains that I spend more time with my laptop than I do with her; and my favorite toy is an iPod. But, of course, I am far from alone. Most of us can recognize and appreciate the great joys and benefits of the digital age.

Yet, regardless of these joys and benefits, the fact remains that we are part of a vastly overstimulated culture that churns out infinitely more images, data and information than any of us has the slightest idea what to do with. We are stuffed to the gills with mental junk food that bloats the mind but leaves the soul malnourished. Indeed, despite our abundance of wealth, food, information, technological wizardry and labor-saving devices, we are left with a yearning that no amount of knowledge or possessions can satisfy.

Thomas Moore, in *Care of the Soul*, argues that the malady of our society is a "loss of soul," and that this is implicated in all our troubles, whether individual or social. When the soul is neglected, he says, "it doesn't just go away; it appears symptomatically in obsessions, addictions, violence, and loss of meaning." The temptation is to isolate these symptoms or to try to eradicate them one by one, "but the root problem is that we have lost our wisdom about the soul, even our interest in it."

Addictions are, I believe, a substitute for spirituality; they are misguided attempts to transcend the aching reality of hungry souls. Our addiction as a society to consumerism, to constant stimulation of the senses, to a relentless buzz of information, to substance abuse, to a culture of "more," "bigger," "better," is in fact a distorted response to an inner longing. Spiritual yearning has been assuaged with artificial stimulants.

The gentle wisdom of the twenty-third psalm points us in a different direction: "He makes me lie down in green pastures." To those who feel stressed and overstimulated, who sense that the "system," like a great parasite, has sucked them dry of creative vitality, the shepherd-God says, "Lie down in the lush meadows of my love. Cease your feverish activity. Rest awhile. Recharge your spirit. Regain equilibrium. Let me replenish your soul."

Like sheep, people get hungry, thirsty and tired, but our hunger is for more than food, and the rest we need is more than physical relaxation. Our souls get hungry, thirsty and tired. In *The Clown in the Belfry*, Frederick Buechner says that it is often that sense of inner emptiness that lets us know we have souls in the first place.

There is nothing that the world has to give us, there is nothing that we have to give to each other even, that ever

quite fills them. . . . That is what the psalm means by saying that God is like a shepherd, I think. It means that, like
a shepherd he feeds us. He feeds that part of us which is
hungriest and most in need of feeding.

What, then, is the food that the shepherd-God offers?
What are the green pastures for the soul? Real soul food is
this: to know that we are loved without measure, without
limit; that we have always been loved, and always will be.
Fundamentally, this is what I have preached for thirty-seven
years. During that time I have peddled many doctrinal
hobbyhorses, but my underlying message has remained
the same: that God loves people unconditionally. This is
quite simply the core of the gospel, the center of everything.
Everything else that can be said about Christianity is a mere
embellishment of this truth. This alone is the food that our
soul craves: we are loved and wanted.

Sigmund Freud mocked the idea of unconditional love,
arguing that many people are not worthy of love. He is
right, of course. But that only highlights the deeper issue:
that we find it very difficult to disengage love from merit.
We feel that in order to be loved we must deserve to be
loved; we must be worthy. In his wonderful book *Conjectures of a Bystander*, Thomas Merton writes, "God is asking
me, the unworthy, to forget my unworthiness, and that
of my brothers, and dare to advance in the love that has
redeemed us all. And to laugh at the preposterous idea of
'worthiness.'"

The trouble is that the "preposterous idea of worthiness" is frequently propagated in churches. The message
preached may be one of love, but the unspoken message
is one of "Do this," "Don't do that," "Behave like a good
Christian and you will be accepted." And often the churches
that most earnestly proclaim a gospel of grace are the very
ones that practice a Christianity of "worthiness," based on
good works. Rather than being strongholds of generous,

liberating acceptance, churches often end up being bastions of rejection.

The cathartic message of the twenty-third psalm is that I do not have to do anything in order to be loved: "He makes me lie down." More often than is commonly realized, those who enter religious communities, or who become church ministers, are in fact people striving for acceptance. My friend Mike Yaconelli, sadly now deceased, spoke openly of the hours he spent every day doing God's work, but failing to discover the food his soul craved. He talked of being busy, superficial, friendless, afraid and cynical—and unable to understand why.

The turning point for Mike came when he visited the L'Arche community in Toronto, which offers liberating space for the mentally and physically challenged. Within a few days of being in the community he began to see himself in a new light. He realized his whole life was consumed with *doing* rather than *being*, as he describes in *Messy Spirituality*.

> I knew what it meant to believe in Jesus, I didn't know what it meant to be with Jesus. I knew how to talk with Jesus, I didn't know how to sit still long enough to let Jesus talk to me. I found it easy to do the work of God, but I had no idea how to let God work in me. I understood soul-saving, but I was clueless about soul making. I knew how to be busy, but I didn't know how to be still. I could talk about God; I just couldn't listen to God. I felt comfortable with God's people, but I felt uncomfortable alone with God. I was acquainted with the God 'out-there', but I was a complete stranger to the God 'in-here'. I could meet God anywhere . . . except in my heart, in my soul, in my being.

Being silent had never come easy to Mike, but as he quieted down and started listening he heard God saying, "Michael, I'm here. I've been calling you. I've been loving you, but you haven't been listening. Can you hear me, Michael? I love you. I've always loved you. And I've been waiting for you to hear me say that to you. But you've been so busy trying to prove to yourself that you're loved that you haven't heard me."

Mike said he had entirely misunderstood the Christian faith. Many of us have done the same. We have replaced faith with fear. We think we must work for God in order to be accepted. Perhaps we understand with our heads that "grace" means "unmerited favor," but we don't believe it in practice.

Our Christianity, like our culture, is often overstimulated. Amid our frenetic attempts to earn God's—and other people's—approval, we have missed the truth, that the heart of Christianity is a silent letting-go, a yielding of all efforts to please God, a calm realization that nothing can be done to make him love us—he already loves us. "He makes me lie down in green pastures" actually means: "Sit down. Stop trying. Enjoy the feast of divine grace that is set before you."

To some people, this message of God's grace sounds outrageous. As Desmond Tutu observes in *God Has a Dream*, the religious leaders of Jesus's day thought that he was proclaiming "a thoroughly disreputable God with very low standards—any Tom, Dick and Harry, Mary and Jane would soon be jostling with the prim and proper ones." Magnificently, as Bishop Tutu says, this was true. Indeed, Jesus went further, saying that the unlikely ones, the despised ones, the sinners, prostitutes and tax collectors, would in fact precede the "prim and proper ones" into the kingdom of God.

Grace is just a way of describing the kind of love God has toward us, a love based not on worthiness or merit, but on who God is. As Paul Tillich says in *The Shaking of the Foundations*, it is when we are in great pain and restless, when we walk through the dark valley of a meaningless and empty life, when we have violated another life, a life that we loved, or from which we were estranged, when year after year, the longed-for perfection of life does not appear, when the old compulsions reign within us for decades, when despair destroys all joy and courage, that a wave of light breaks into our darkness, and a voice says: "You are accepted. *You are accepted*, accepted by that which is greater than you. . . . Do not try to do anything now. . . . Simply accept the fact that you are accepted!"

Whatever else you believe, believe this: You are loved! You are accepted simply because you are. You are not lumped together with everyone else; you are a person known by name. There are many things that you can know and learn in this age of information, but this is the only thing you really, really need to know: that you are loved, and always will be.

"He leads me beside the still waters"

LEARNING TO BE TRANQUIL

There's a marvelous moment in Monty Python's *Life of Brian*, when Brian is trying to convince his followers that he is not the Messiah. Frustrated with their sheep-like behavior, he shouts out, "You have to think for yourselves! You are all individuals!"

With one voice they all shout back, "We are all individuals!"

Then, after a very brief pause, someone from the back says, "I'm not."

I doubt that any of us really likes the idea of being compared to a sheep. We'd be much happier to be likened to a mighty eagle soaring in the heavens, or a lion majestically roaming the African plains or a dolphin gliding effortlessly through the open seas. Personally, I fancy being a mischievous monkey swinging through the trees.

But who wants to be a sheep? Sheep aren't witty or intelligent or individualistic. Sheep are helpless creatures, vulnerable to predators, prone to getting lost and dependent on others to guide them to food and shelter.

Yet this is how Jesus saw the crowds who followed him. The sight of them moved him to compassion because they were indeed like sheep without a shepherd, harassed and helpless. We may not like to admit it, but there are times for all of us when we are vulnerable, lost and confused—in need of comfort, reassurance and guidance.

Incidents like the suicide bombings in London on July 7, 2005, always produce wonderful human stories. One such story involved a man who called out for help in the darkness and confusion of a bombed-out carriage on the London Underground. "Please help me," he said, "I'm autistic. Does anyone know what that means? I need help." Setting aside fear and the instinct simply to get out as quickly as possible, a woman took the man by the hand and led him through the chaos to safety. The image of the two bedraggled figures emerging from the smoky darkness will live in my mind for a long time: a frightened, thankful man, clinging to his good shepherd in the midst of turmoil.

"The Lord is my shepherd. . . . He leads me. . . ." One common argument against religion is that faith is a moral crutch for the weak-minded. Setting aside the fact that many religious figures have been anything but weak-minded wimps—St. Paul, Gandhi, Muhammad, Desmond Tutu and Mother Teresa to name but a few—the truth is, we all need to lean on something or someone at some time or other. While having much sympathy for those who feel they cannot believe in anything beyond the purely material realm, I have always felt repelled by the macho atheism that clings resolutely to human self-sufficiency. In life's darker moments, the vast majority of us invoke the name of God, even if as an expletive—which is often a prayer in itself: "Oh, Jesus . . . !" "God Almighty . . . !" "God help us!"

"He leads me beside the still waters." The images that normally accompany this verse are those of glassy alpine lakes surrounded by majestic mountain peaks reflected in the water. Such scenes are magnificent, but they are a long way from the hectic, messy lives most of us lead. If still waters equate with trouble-free lives and the absence of

43

difficulty, darkness and loss, then the experience of tranquility is out of our reach.

The realization that trusting in God did not guarantee a smooth life dawned on me at an early age. My father was a devoted Christian who read his Bible and prayed every day; but he was disabled and lived with constant pain and discomfort. Nothing came easy to my dad. He struggled constantly to eke out a meager living for his family, and he was constantly frustrated with his physical limitations. And as we didn't have a bathroom, he had to bathe himself from a bowl in front of the fire, requiring a lot of help. I can't imagine the embarrassment and humiliation that was a routine part of his existence.

Life was hard for Fred Tomlinson. But he instilled in my brother and me a simple sense of trust in God. Religion for him wasn't about a divine Father Christmas, who took away the nasty bits of life, replacing them with glittering gifts of straightforward answers to prayers, miracle cures or instant provisions. His faith was all about a shepherd-God who imparted a sense of peace and tranquility in the midst of hardship, who instilled the kind of self-worth that enabled a seriously disabled man to achieve things that many people with two good legs never achieve.

I grew up in a home where the notion of a shepherd-God who leads us beside still waters meant that I knew I was loved and accepted come what may, that beyond the fluctuations and seeming randomness of life a deeper pattern could be discerned—I knew I could experience divine peace, whatever happened, because my mom and dad did.

Such tranquility stands in stark contrast to the frenzied activity of our age, where personal worth is often linked to what we do, where we are headed or the things we possess. Yet, despite our abundance of technological gadgetry and labor-saving devices, the burden of living has never weighed more heavily on the human soul. So much, it seems, is required of us: so much pressure to win our silly inconsequential games, so little time to accommodate the people and things that truly matter. Marcia Hornok's ironic rewriting of Psalm 23 sums the situation up perfectly:

> The clock is my dictator; I shall not rest.
> It makes me lie down only when exhausted.
> It leads me to deep depression.
> It hounds my soul.
> It leads me in circles of frenzy for activity's sake.
> Even though I run frantically from task to task, I
>   will never get it all done,
> For my 'ideal' is with me.
> Deadlines and my need for approval, they drive
>   me.
> They demand performance from me, beyond the
>   limits of my schedule.
> They anoint my head with migraines.
> My in-basket overflows.
> Surely fatigue and time pressure shall follow me all
>   the days of my life.
> And I will dwell in the bonds of frustration forever.

How many of us live like this: frequently exhausted and depressed, never feeling as though we're on top of things, always stressed, always trying to catch up? For some the pressure is associated with work, for others it's about the strain of running a house or bringing up children; for many it revolves around finance, or shaky relationships, or concern about the future. Any of these can feel like a mini-tsunami about to engulf us and swallow us up.

To those of us who feel this way, the psalmist offers hope and reassurance: the shepherd-God leads us beside still waters. The chaos that threatens to overwhelm us can be stilled, just as Jesus calmed the stormy Sea of Galilee. We can know peace. But how?

45

First, we need to make some space for peace, to create a little sanctuary in our frenetic lives. A good place to start is to set aside a small amount of time in each day. Even if it is only five minutes to begin with, you will soon see the difference. Decide on a place where you can be free from distractions. A corner can become sacred space by gathering some objects on a table or shelf: a candle, a small icon or picture, a cross, a special stone. Then spend a few minutes relaxing and meditating.

The Worth Abbey website offers the following five tips for meditation:

- Find a quiet place free from distraction.
- Sit with your limbs uncrossed and with a straight back, hands in your lap.
- Simply breathe at regular speed but breathe deeply and relax.
- Close your eyes and think of a beautiful scene from the natural world.
- Take a simple phrase and repeat it continuously in time with your breathing.

Yet however vital it is for us to create space and personal sanctuary, we can never truly know inner peace and tranquility on our own. In Hebrew, the term for "still waters" literally means "waters of rest and relaxation," and to know that kind of stillness, we need friends and family. Meals are a perfect setting for cultivating a peaceful atmosphere. I believe every meal can be a sacrament of peace. Yet in our increasingly individualized, fast food culture, meals have increasingly become utilitarian events rather than celebrations of fun and friendship that feed the soul as well as the body. A culture of individualism produces tense, edgy lives; a communion of kindred spirits produces rootedness, security and tranquility.

One of the greatest clues to tranquil living is contained in Reinhold Niebuhr's famous prayer for serenity, which is now associated with Alcoholics Anonymous:

> God grant me the serenity to accept the things I
>   cannot change;
> courage to change the things I can;
> and wisdom to know the difference.

The simplicity and profoundness of this prayer is awesome. Peace must never be confused with passivity. There are things in life and in the world that we *can* do something about, that we *can* change; and we must have the courage to do so if we want to know inner peace. But there are also things that we cannot change, things that are entirely beyond our control that we must learn to accept peacefully.

In the less well-known part of Niebuhr's prayer, he goes further:

> Living one day at a time; enjoying one moment at a time; accepting hardships as the pathway to peace; taking, as He did, this sinful world as it is, not as I would have it; trusting that He will make all things right if I surrender to His will; that I may be reasonably happy in this life and supremely happy with Him forever in the next. Amen.

We live in an alarming world, a "turning world"; but there is, as T. S. Eliot says, a "still point of the turning world," and it is at that still point that we find assurance that there is a pattern to our random world, that there is meaning to our meager existence, that someone cares. Finally, tranquility is the result of trust in a loving God, of hope that there is a bigger picture, of charity that musters the courage to reach out and work for the peace and tranquility of others.

"He restores my soul"

Finding fresh energy

Sheep don't often hit the headlines. Although, amazingly, during the past decade two sheep have done just that. The first, of course, was Dolly, the famous cloned sheep, and the other was a New Zealand Merino ram known as Shrek.

It seems as though this particular animal took a dislike to the annual ritual of shearing. So it hid among the rocky caves of the ranch, managing to avoid detection for six years. During that time the renegade ram grew the most colossal fleece anyone has ever seen. When the farmer finally spotted the animal he didn't even recognize it as a sheep at all. He later described it as looking like a giant woolly slug, with its nose barely protruding and its feet only just visible. The ram was soon named Shrek, after the ogre from the famous film.

Shrek the ram became a celebrity. The whole world was fascinated that a sheep could have escaped capture for so long. Shrek's fleece weighed no less than 60 pounds—enough to make 20 men's suits—and fast became a sought-after commodity. It was auctioned on eBay for $50,000, in support of a children's charity.

No one knows how Shrek survived. His enormous fleece could easily have entangled or trapped him, and he made it through the bitter winters with very little food available.

Shrek's extraordinary tale of survival would be worth a fortune if he could only tell it to someone. Imagine what the tabloids would pay for his exclusive—and then there are the film rights! Yet it's an exceptional story that simply proves the rule: sheep need a shepherd.

Shrek was lucky. A couple of years ago I came across the remains of a less fortunate sheep at our cottage in Yorkshire. In a neglected corner of the garden, cut off by a forest of weeds and nettles, there are the remains of an outside toilet. Having clambered over the wall into the garden, the sheep had apparently maneuvered its way into the tiny outhouse—probably in pursuit of a juicy tuft of grass just inside the door. But having got in, it clearly couldn't get out again. I found its remains when I finally got around to clearing that bit of the garden.

Actually, although the film of Shrek the renegade ram would portray him as a "black sheep," a nonconformist, free-thinking rebel who cut away from the flock to carve out a different life and identity, the reality is that he probably just got lost. Sheep do that. They fancy that bit of green grass over there, beyond the hedge, in the next field—"the grass is always greener" and all that. No wonder we're likened to sheep.

I have no idea how Shrek felt during those long, hard winters, out on the rocky slopes alone; but I do know what it's like to feel lost. It's frightening. We lose our bearings. Everything is unfamiliar, perhaps threatening. We have no idea which way to go. We are confused and disoriented. We feel panicky. Alone. Our energy dissipates.

My mom always used to tell me that if I was lost, the best thing to do was to stand still. "I'll always find you if you just stay in one place," she would say. It was good advice—unlike the guidance one young woman was given by her grandfather, who said, "If you're lost, just keep turning left." I'm sure there must be some logic there somewhere, but in reality it meant that his granddaughter spent two

51

hours going round and round Palmer's Green one day when she was trying to find her way from the M1 to our house in Holloway!

But we don't have to wander the wastelands of North London to be lost. Sometimes we can feel lost in our own homes, or when friends surround us. The feeling of being lost comes from that lonely, empty space that sometimes opens up within. It can happen when we receive bad news about our health or the health of someone we love, when we feel unexpectedly let down by somebody we trust, when our job is suddenly taken away, when we appear stupid in front of people we respect, when someone close to us dies. In all of these and many other circumstances, we can be heard to say, "I just feel lost!"

But often it is simply in the midst of life's ordinariness that we feel lost. The sheer busyness and stress of living cause us to lose our bearings and lose sight of what truly matters to us. "He restores my soul" literally means, "He renews my life." The soul is that essential energy at the core of our being; it is our life energy. The soul is not some disembodied bit of us, it is the sum total of who we are as a person; it is the essence of our being.

When we feel lost, when we lose the sense of who we are or where we fit, when we feel isolated or lonely or be-reaved: our life energy diminishes, our soul shrinks. When we become bogged down with worry and anxiety, when we feel inadequate and vulnerable: our creativity dries up, our imagination is stifled, our soul fades. When the grime of an overcompetitive, self-seeking culture clings to our consciousness, when we get trapped on the treadmill of mediocrity, when we mistake the trivial and inconsequential for the truly essential, when we are so engulfed in the here and now that we lose sight of the beyond: then our sense of wonder is lost, our soul shrivels.

I did once have the pleasure of rescuing a real lost sheep. My wife and I were walking through a bracing wind on the bleak wintry Swaledale moors when we spotted a sheep on its back in a hollow. Farmers would describe the sheep as "cast": stuck on its back and unable to get up without assistance. Initially, a cast sheep will thrash around frantically, trying to right itself; but eventually its energy drains away, as does the blood from its legs. Depending on the conditions, the sheep will die in a matter of hours. So you can imagine the buzz I felt as I grasped this particular sheep by its fleece, spun it over and watched it wobble a little and then walk away.

"He restores my soul." He puts me on my feet again and re-energizes my whole being. He restores my life energy. But how does he do it? How does the shepherd-God restore our soul?

Often, divine help comes in the form of another human being, whether friend or stranger. The Swaledale sheep and I had never met, but I saved its life. Ultimately, it doesn't really matter whom God uses to restore our souls—but often it does have to be someone other than ourselves. Help may come from a health professional or a counselor, from a friend or work colleague, from a stranger on the bus or a magazine vendor. A woman I know received life-changing wisdom from someone she happened to chat with over a coffee in Starbucks. She doesn't even know his name. The parable of the Good Samaritan teaches us that help can come from the most unexpected places. But it is very important that we learn to ask for help. In the words of U2: "Sometimes you can't make it on your own." So swallow your pride, take the hand that is offered and draw upon the energy of compassion.

Many people find that being in church services restores their soul—though I guess that depends on the church! A woman told me recently that coming to church makes her feel clean again. "It's as if I pick up some of the grime from living in a greedy, grabbing world," she said, "but being here helps me shake it off; refocus things. I get a fresh glimpse of what matters. I feel human again."

To take part in prayerful liturgy is to place one's life in the context of prayer. It is to reframe one's life: to redraw the parameters of what is important, what is possible. Simply being there allows our soul to breathe, to draw in the breath of a different place. The spirit, if not the mouth, begins to mutter the words, "The Lord is my shepherd. . . . He renews my life."

It's not by coincidence that art and music have always played such an important part in religious experience; these also restore the soul. When doctrines and creeds feel pointless and empty, when the words of preachers sail right over the head, it is often the choir, or the stained glass images, or an icon, or the majesty of architecture, or the sound of an organ that revitalizes the spirit. Sometimes, just sitting in an empty church, surrounded by timeless beauty, can be enough to restore inner serenity.

But it isn't just specifically religious art that replenishes the soul. So-called "secular" art can have the same effect. Bono talks about how the honesty of John Lennon, the baroque language of Bob Dylan and Leonard Cohen and the open throat of Al Green and Stevie Wonder touch some deep inner part of him. "When I hear these singers," he says, "I am reconnected to a part of me I have no explanation for . . . my 'soul,' I guess." Ambling around an art gallery, listening to music, watching a film, reading a book—or indeed singing, writing or painting something of our own—can easily become a soul-restoring experience.

Friendship is another of God's powerful healing gifts. Decades of research have shown that friendship is good for our health. People who have friends have lower death rates. They recover from illness faster. They have lower rates of certain diseases. But it's not just our physical well-being that is helped by having friends: friendship also energizes the soul. Couples are often referred to as "soul mates," but I think everyone should have soul mates—truly "best friends." Thomas Moore describes a soul mate as someone to whom we feel profoundly connected, as though the friendship seems less the product of intentional effort and more of a gift or a divine grace. We sometimes talk about "clicking" with someone. This sort of connection is profoundly powerful in restoring the soul. It's the kind of relationship that reorients, that heals our feelings of being lost and re-establishes our sense of being "at home."

Fun and laughter are also good for the soul. All work and no play may make Dave a dull boy, but it also diminishes Dave's spiritual well-being. Playfulness is a divine attribute and a gift for the welfare of the soul. Sadly, we have tended to replace genuine playfulness with a leisure industry, where all the stress and burden of living is perpetuated if not multiplied. Rather than restoring the soul, so-called leisure often adds to our fears and anxieties. Joy and laughter are a natural consequence of living in the presence of the shepherd-God. Truly spiritual people are playful people who recognize that joy, smiles and laughter open the doors to God's kingdom.

If the Lord is your shepherd, then in the great scheme of things—you matter. You are created by One who counts the hairs on your head, who cares about sparrows, who tracks down lost sheep and calls every person in a crowd by name. God re-energizes the soul as the sun replenishes the earth. Relax. Rest in the care of the One who knows you fully and loves you completely.

Let me finish with a Japanese interpretation of Psalm 23:

> The Lord is my Pace-setter; I shall not rush.
> He makes me stop and rest for quiet intervals.
> He provides me with images of stillness, that re-
> store my serenity; He leads me in ways of effi-
> ciency through calmness of mind,
> And His guidance is peace.

Even though I have a great many things to accomplish each day, I will not fret, for His presence is here.

His timelessness, His all importance, will keep me in balance.

He prepares refreshment and renewal in the midst of my activity by anointing my mind with His oils of tranquility.

My cup of joyous energy overflows!

Surely harmony and effectiveness shall be the fruits of my hours,

For I shall walk in the peace of my Lord, and dwell in His house forever.

                                         Toki Miyashina

"He leads me in right
paths for his name's sake"

GOD DOWN EVERY ROAD

Albert Einstein once boarded a train in Princeton, New Jersey, bound for Boston. Upon finding a seat he immediately started fumbling for his ticket, which he couldn't find anywhere. Noticing Einstein's frantic search, the conductor reassured him: "Everyone on this train knows who you are, Professor Einstein. I don't need to see your ticket." While looking relieved, Einstein carried on hunting for the missing ticket. When the conductor came back along the train he saw the renowned scientist on his hands and knees looking under the seat. He tapped Einstein on the shoulder and said, "Please, Professor, don't worry about the ticket. I am quite sure you have one somewhere." To which Einstein replied, "No, no. You don't understand. I need the ticket because I don't know where I am going."

I am sure that Einstein was on a busy lecture tour covering many locations, but there is still something perversely comforting about the idea that one of the greatest minds in history could be so befuddled as to forget where he was going on a train journey. There may be some hope for the rest of us, after all.

Yet, on the greater journey of life itself, most of us share some of Einstein's confusion; now and then we too experience feelings of being lost, and question where we are headed. In the normal course of events these feelings are buried under a mountain of routine activities, but in times of bereavement or depression, or through the breakdown of a relationship, or under the threat of serious illness or around a significant birthday, they can surface with unsettling persistence.

A couple of years ago a parishioner in his mid-thirties came to see me. He was a heroin addict who had contracted HIV through using dirty needles. He was very frightened of dying, but avoided thinking about it, mainly by getting another hit—then another, and another and another. In a rare moment of sobriety he rang my doorbell, desperate to tell someone how he felt. After hearing his informal confession, I prayed with him and read the twenty-third psalm. He warmed to the thought that God was his shepherd and asked me to pray that he would find the right paths spoken about in the psalm. "There's got to be some better paths than the ones I've gone down," he said.

Like all journeys, the journey of life involves choices. Every road has junctions in it, and every junction requires a decision, a choice. And choices can be very difficult to make. Sadly, this man found the right choices very hard to make. His body was discovered in an underground car park frequented by drug users. He had taken an overdose. Perhaps he thought that taking his life was the best choice he had. Perhaps this was the only way he felt he could escape the dark valley he walked through every day. I officiated at his funeral, entrusting him to the shepherd-God he had cried out to in my study some months earlier. I believe God received him into the bosom of his love, despite the addiction he just couldn't kick.

Choices cannot be avoided. Life is a series of choices, and there is no way around them. To avoid a choice is to make a choice. On the journey of life, we will travel down one road or another. The only question is, Which will it be? The thought of this can drive some people crazy, because none of us want to make bad choices or wrong choices. None of us want to go down the wrong road. And while some people take comfort from the statement, "He leads me in right paths for his name's sake," others find it adds to the problem, because it simply begs the question, How can I know that I am walking on the right path? How can I be sure that this is the road God is leading me down?

Much of this problem stems from the "divine blueprint" approach to Christian spirituality: the idea that God has some perfect plan for our lives mapped out to the last detail. Those who adopt this outlook are frequently driven by the neurotic fear of getting "it" wrong. Questions like, *How can I know which voice is God's? Where is God leading? Which is the right way to go? What is the Lord trying to say?* easily become an obsession, leading to chronic anxiety, fear and loss of self-esteem. Life develops into a cosmic game of snakes and ladders—make one wrong move and you will slither out of God's will. Countless Christians fall prey to this kind of thinking, constantly afraid of missing God's best for their lives, or feeling like second-class citizens because they think they have indeed failed to attain God's best.

I once counseled a lovely woman who had been abused in every imaginable way by a violent, bullying husband. Her body bore the scars where he had stubbed out his cigarettes in her flesh. Eventually she left him, for her own safety and that of her children. Years later she met a man who loved her, but her church leaders told her that remarriage was out of the question if she wanted to remain with God's best for her life. Desperately afraid of displeasing God, she turned down the offer of marriage, choosing instead a life of frustration and loneliness. She had married the "wrong" man, taken the wrong fork in the road, and now she must live with the consequences.

One of the best parts of my job as a vicar is to explode false images of God, images like the one this woman had been given. The "gospel" that scarred her life with feelings of guilt and failure, and which condemned her to years of isolation, is not worthy of the name of God. It is a distortion of the Christian message. Yet, sadly, it is all that many Christians know. The doctrine of "God's second best" is in fact a travesty, an affront to the One who says, "Behold, I make all things new." The shepherd-God is the lover of our souls, not some petty religious functionary, who scrutinizes people's lives to see when they put a foot wrong.

Yes, there are forks in the road. There are choices to be made, and some choices are much better than others. But here is the good news: God is down every road. God owns all the roads, as Craig Barnes puts it in his inspiring book *Searching for Home: Spirituality for Restless Souls*. We need to understand, he says, that our lives will end up in the right place not because of our good choices, but because of the choice God made to love us. "And this love is waiting for you at either fork in the road."

But surely some roads are just wrong, someone will say. And of course this is correct, but God is down those roads too, as the prodigal son discovered when he encountered grace (or at least started to encounter it) at the bottom of a pig trough. C. S. Lewis once said that God uses all the wrong roads to get us to the right places. Most of us "stumble into grace," as Emmylou Harris puts it in one of her songs.

Rabbi Harold Kushner explains that the term "right paths," used in Psalm 23, literally means "roundabout ways that end up in the right direction." God takes our wrong choices, our bad decisions, our roundabout routes, and shifts them in the right direction—if we will allow him to do so.

Walking on right paths has nothing to do with following some divine blueprint for our lives—living in the "right" place, marrying the "right" person, following the "right" career. And it has nothing to do with being perfect people who never screw up. Fundamentally, it is about getting in touch with the God who always loves us; it is about gain-ing wisdom by understanding what God is like; it is about learning to trust God.

The twenty-third psalm is all about learning to trust God, the shepherd-God who will never leave our side. It offers no shortcuts around the nasty bits of life, no foolproof methods for attaining a perfect existence. What it does promise is the assurance that even in the nasty parts, even with our own imperfections, deep down, all is well. Frederick Buechner reminds us in *The Clown in the Belfry* that righteousness is not just about *doing* right, but about *being* right:

> . . . being right with God, trusting the deep-down right-
> ness of the life God has created for us and in us. . . . We are
> shepherded by the knowledge that though all is far from
> right with any world you and I know anything about, all
> is right deep down. All will be right at last.

Maybe you are about to get married or enter a partner-ship. Maybe you have babies or are about to have your first child. Maybe you are facing a career change, buying a house or thinking about some other challenging shift in your life. Maybe, on the other hand, you feel that decisions are being forced upon you: a loved one has been taken away, you are facing redundancy, illness threatens or money is running out. Or maybe life is secure, predictable, boring, and you are looking for a new adventure. Maybe you feel it is too late for new journeys. Take heart: place your trust in the shepherd-God, who will lead you in right paths for his name's sake.

There is a lovely Dr. Seuss book called *Oh, the Places You'll Go!* It's a story of new beginnings that works for people of all ages. It talks about the choices we make throughout our lives. You may go up and down good and bad streets. You may experience success or failure. Sometimes you will end up in what Dr. Seuss calls "the waiting place." You will be stuck there, waiting for your hair to grow, or for the phone to ring, or for the path to become clear for you. The point of the story is that we should not be afraid to try new things. We should not be afraid of making choices. We discover who we are in the process of going forward, not sitting still.

Once we place our trust in the shepherd-God instead of trusting in our own ability to scrutinize God's mind, once we understand that God owns all the roads, that his love will not let us go, that he sticks with us even in our moments of stupidity, then we are free to make better choices—without the anxiety that our souls are on the line every time we make a decision.

"EVEN THOUGH I WALK THROUGH THE DARKEST VALLEY"

PASSING THROUGH THE DARK VALLEY

The only time I ever experience real darkness is at our cottage in Yorkshire. It's a mile and a half to the nearest road, and even that has no streetlights. So, apart from moonlit nights, if we wake up in the dead of night when the fire has finally gone out, it is impossible to see anything at all. I know it's an old cliché, but I still find myself moving my hand in front of my face just to convince myself how dark it is.

I confess I am not comfortable with darkness—my wife is much better with it than me. So why I find such pleasure in going to an isolated cottage with no electricity is anybody's guess. If I have to go to the bathroom in the middle of the night, I tend to move as quickly as possible, spooking myself with the thought that someone is just behind me. It's at that point that I wish I had closed the doors of the rooms I have to pass; each door feels like a dark hole with monsters about to leap out at me. Even my flashlight offers small comfort because it creates so many moving shadows. And there is something sinister about shadows. They suggest threatening images and give the feeling that something is about to engulf me. What a relief to open the bedroom door and get back into the familiar bed.

Why is it that shadows and darkness are so scary and disturbing? Ultimately, it is because we link darkness to the grave. Death is associated with darkness and night as life is associated with daylight. It is a connection that is deeply embedded in our consciousness. Our ancient forebears thought of death as a twilight underworld, a place of inescapable gloom where people faded into shadows of their former selves. And this is reflected in the Old Testament notion of Sheol, which is portrayed as a comfortless place beneath the earth, where both the bad and the good, slave and king, must go after death to sleep in oblivion. The hope of God-fearing Jews was, in the words of Psalm 49, that "God will ransom my soul from the power of Sheol, for he will receive me."

Death has always troubled human beings, because we are the only creatures with an awareness that we are going to die. The writer of Psalm 39 was acutely aware of his mortality. His life, he says, is a few handbreadths, a mere breath or puff of wind. "I am your passing guest," he says to God, "an alien, like all my forebears." Some may see the knowledge of our own mortality as a curse, but it goes with the territory of being human. Knowing that we are mortal brings a sense of focus to our lives. We know that our time is limited; that we can't revisit our life and make it different. This causes some people to say, "What the hell . . . eat, drink and be merry, for tomorrow I'll die," but it inspires others to make wise choices so that their lives will count.

Nowadays we have a million distractions to guide our thoughts away from the certainty of death. Many buy into the myth of immortality and eternal youth, sometimes at a great cost. Even when we do encounter death, the funeral industry helps us to maintain a "safe" distance from the actualities and physical details of death. This was not always the case. I can still recall the times when the "chapel of rest" was the front parlor, and when it was not unusual for relatives to wash the body of their deceased loved one. The shift toward a more hands-off approach to death is signaled by the fact that we now have "funeral directors" instead of "undertakers." And while we can choose, if we wish, to actually press the button, igniting the burners that transform our loved one's remains to a heap of ash, most people would see it as rather macabre. Instead, we keep our distance, and stave off the lurking fascination with what happens when the coffin goes through those little doors from the chapel.

Yet for all our efforts to detach ourselves from the realities of death, the dark valley of grief and loss is inescapable. People handle the experience in many different ways, but I have yet to visit the home of a mourner without sensing the shadow of death. We may live in a more sanitized society, but there is no way around the pain of knowing that someone we love is gone, never to return.

Yet, despite the fact that Psalm 23 is commonly seen as the funeral psalm, the original Hebrew text never mentions death. The phrase "shadow of death" is better translated as "deep darkness." There are many dark valleys in life, not all directly linked to death—relationship breakdown, debt and financial worry, dashed hopes, a sense of failure, depression or prolonged illness. Yet perhaps the translators of the King James Bible had it right: perhaps all of life's dark valleys do have the shadow of death hanging over them. Maybe these are all mini-deaths that remind us of our ultimate fate.

But the great message of the twenty-third psalm is that valleys are to be passed *through*, not occupied as a home. We are not meant to live under the shadow of death throughout our lives. Sadly, however, some people do. We talk about people having a shadow or cloud hanging over them. Sometimes we can see the gloom in their eyes or in their body language.

C. S. Lewis's devastating grief at the death of his wife, Joy, is marvelously portrayed in the film *Shadowlands*. For months Lewis was inconsolable and quite unable to recognize the depths of grief in his two stepsons. His brother, Warnie, could see what was happening and chided Lewis about the effect his grief was having on the boys. But grief can be very blind. Eventually, Lewis emerged from the shadow of his wife's death and wrote the little masterpiece *A Grief Observed*. We should never diminish the pain of the bereaved, but it is possible, essential even, to pass through the valley and move on.

Three years ago I buried a man who had suddenly died at age forty-three. His widow was heartbroken. There were still so many dreams to follow, so many adventures to pursue. I had no words that could help. I sat with her in silence. It just wasn't fair. A year ago she was still devastated, unable to work, to play, to allow people into her life. But today she is moving on. She still feels the pain, still misses him dreadfully. But she is rebuilding her life as he would want her to.

Psalm 23 presents no magic answers to those who grieve or who suffer for any other reason. What it offers is the assurance that we need never face the pain alone. And my experience with grief is that God never rushes in with torrents of wise words. You just know he is there, ready to absorb all your anger and expletives.

Sometimes we need to know that it is all right to move on, to know that by doing so we are not hurting the deceased or their memory. I like the fact that the Jewish tradition provides a pause five times a year, on the four holiday seasons and on the anniversary of a person's death, to remember the departed. This provides a framework to express *and contain* grief. Christianity offers no formal process of grief after the funeral, which is a shame. Maybe we Christians should learn a new custom from our Jewish friends.

69

One survivor of the London bombings provides an awe-inspiring story of someone who is determined to move through his particular dark valley. The thirty-seven-year-old south London man had his lower leg blown clean off. He says he knew it had gone right away. Yet as he lay in the hospital bed, preparing to be fitted with an artificial limb, he betrayed no bitterness whatsoever. "If I allow myself to have a bad day then they [the bombers] have won that one day from me. . . . I'm looking at myself as being one of the lucky ones. My life still remains here, I can still move on with it."

Psalm 23 makes no attempt to sidestep evil, or to pretend that life will be trouble-free. Terrible things happen—to good people as well as bad. Everyone we know will die one day. We will die. The psalm does not tiptoe around that fact. Its message is that human existence has meaning, that pain and suffering are not the end, that there is a heaven, that it matters to someone whether we live or die and that there is a way through life's dark valleys.

At worst, the message of trust and contentment in the twenty-third psalm can produce a "pie in the sky" mentality; the sort of passivity that allows oppression and injustice free rein on the basis that "heaven is just around the corner." But this is to misinterpret the psalm, which should rather create the sort of inner peace that enables us to cast cares aside and confront prejudice, cruelty, tyranny and unfairness in the name of the Good Shepherd who sacrificed his very life to meet head-on the sources of evil and injustice in our world.

Yet the ultimate framework for all our social initiatives and every effort toward creating a more just world is the realization that death is not the end. As Bob Dylan puts it:

> When all that you hold sacred
> falls down and does not mend,
> and all your dreams have vanished,

and you don't know what's up the bend,
just remember that death is not the end.

Having a vision of the cosmos that reaches beyond shadows, dark valleys and even death itself enables us to gain a different perspective on the troubles and trials of this life. I recently read about a man who finally lost his battle with cancer. But even as he struggled, even as he passed through the valley of the shadow of death, he felt the presence of the Good Shepherd. At his funeral some words were printed on the back of the service sheet:

Cancer is so limited . . .
It cannot cripple love,
It cannot shatter hope,
It cannot corrode faith,
It cannot eat away peace,
It cannot destroy confidence,
It cannot kill friendship,
It cannot shut out memories,
It cannot silence courage,
It cannot invade the soul,
It cannot reduce eternal life,
It cannot quench the spirit,
It cannot lessen the power of the resurrection.

One of the most impressive features of accounts people give of near-death experiences is the great similarity in what they describe. Having studied the subject quite carefully, I find these accounts quite compelling. It's interesting that rather than talking about a dark valley, people describe a tunnel with a great light at the end, where they are welcomed by someone they had known on earth. The overwhelming message is that death need not be frightening.

There is a line in Kahlil Gibran's book *The Prophet* where he speaks of those who stand with their backs to the sun—to whom the sun is but a caster of shadows. But what is a shadow? A shadow is caused when something blocks out the light. As Rabbi Kushner reminds us, there cannot be shadows without the sun shining, "and the shadow of death cannot blight our lives unless the experience of death comes between us and the sun."

It's all a matter of perspective, and perspective depends on which way we are facing. The twenty-third psalm points us toward the sun, toward the One whose love and acceptance is infinitely greater than any shadow cast by death. As we sink in the waters of our own doubt and anxiety, Jesus holds out his hand, saying, "Do not be afraid, it is I." Remember, death is not the end.

A poet from Mexico, Amado Nervo, wrote this prayer to the shepherd expressing profound trust.

> Shepherd, I bless you for what you give me.
> If nothing you give me, I also so bless you.
> I follow you laughing, through roses and thorns;
> Through brambles and thistles, I joyously follow.
> With you when there's plenty, with you when I
>   want.
> Still always with you.

"I FEAR NO EVIL;
FOR YOU ARE WITH ME"

Is there anybody there?

On one of my first preaching trips abroad, I recall staying in a hotel and feeling a bit lost without my wife. Sitting in the room, wondering what to do with the next couple of hours before going to bed, I picked up the Gideon Bible and started thumbing through it. At the beginning of a Gideon Bible there are some tips on how to find your way around the Bible, and where to look for specific guidance if you are, say, depressed, lonely or afraid. Psalm 23 is suggested for anyone who feels lonely, so I took a look and was duly cheered—not by the familiar words of the psalm but by the advice someone had scrawled in the margin that said: "And if you're still lonely, call Roxanne!"

None of us wants to be alone. And sometimes we will go to great lengths to ensure that we are not alone, or at least to ensure that we do not feel alone. We are frightened of being alone. It is a basic human need to feel the presence of another. Without that presence, we can easily wither on the inside. With it, we can be virtually invincible.

There is a story about a little boy, just starting his first term at elementary school, who is asked, along with all the other children, to speak for a few moments on "What I want to be when I grow up." After several nervous presentations from his classmates, the little boy stands up, looking surprisingly confident. "When I grow up I'm going to be a lion tamer," he says, emphatically. "I'll have lots of scary lions who will roar when I get into the cage." Suddenly he pauses, clearly contemplating what it might be like to enter a cage of roaring lions, then adds, "But of course, I'll have my mommy with me."

The truly big question in life is: is there anybody there? Is there a "mommy" in the cosmos? Does it matter to anyone what happens to me? In the big scheme of things, does my life matter? The twenty-third psalm offers a resounding "Yes!" It says life may be frightening, with dark valleys, dangers and death, but it will be okay because I am not alone: "The Lord is my shepherd."

It is time to make an observation about the grammatical structure of Psalm 23. The name of the shepherd is uttered just twice: abruptly at the beginning of the poem—"The Lord is my shepherd"—and at the end—"I shall dwell in the house of the Lord forever" (italics added). As Walter Brueggemann points out in *The Message of the Psalms*, this gives the impression that the psalm—like a trustful life—is lived fully in the presence of this name, which sets the parameters for life itself.

Then, at the center of the psalm, the writer makes a sudden and significant shift. He stops talking about God as a "he" and starts addressing God as "you," or "thou" in the famous King James Version.

> The Lord is my shepherd, I shall not want.
> *He* makes me lie down in green pastures;
> *He* leads me beside still waters;
> *He* restores my soul.
> *He* leads me in right paths for *his* name's sake.
> Even though I walk through the darkest valley,
> I fear no evil; for *you* are with me;
> *Your* rod and *your* staff—they comfort me (italics added).

The writer makes a shift from reciting beliefs to saying a prayer, from rehearsing information *about* God to entering into a conversation *with* him. It is the difference between theology, which discusses God, and spirituality, which experiences God. Or to put it in more colloquial terms, it is the difference between reading about programs in the TV guide and actually watching them on the television.

Actually, theology and spirituality belong together, as they do in this psalm. And churches should be places where theology and spirituality exist side by side, where God is indeed talked about, but also talked to. More than anything else, a church is a house of prayer, a place where our vision and perspective on life can be refocused by talking with and listening to God. Our circumstances may not change as a result, our lives may not become any easier or our dark valleys less dark, but something important happens when we pray: our lives are reoriented.

One aspect of this reorientation is the fresh realization that we are never alone, and that our minds, therefore, need not be governed by fear. Fear is a devastating and destructive emotion. Fear paralyzes the mind. Fear crushes creativity. Fear causes mistrust in relationships. Fear isolates. Fear causes anxiety. Fear damages health. Fear limits possibilities. Fear cripples the mind and the imagination. Fear prohibits adventure. Fear creates panic. Fear prevents decisions being made. Fear puts life on hold.

One of the things Jesus said most commonly throughout his ministry was: "Do not fear." "Do not be afraid." He was acutely aware of what fear does to people; that it destroys faith and stalls the process of people hearing God or receiving from God. It distorts people's whole understanding of God, and of themselves.

Of course, minor fears are part of life. We all feel nerves when we are stepping into the limelight, or into the unknown; we all have minor anxieties about life's uncertainties. But real fear and panic skews our sense of reality and creates isolation and alienation. It then becomes very difficult to feel a connection with God or with other people. Fear and trust cannot inhabit the same space.

Sometimes we can rationalize our way through fear. We can analyze what is going on and convince ourselves that the fear is ungrounded. At other times we feel too panicky, or the sense of danger is too intense for us to reason our way through. Yet, so often, what we really need is the reassurance of someone else's presence.

Madeleine L'Engle gives a wonderful account of how she instinctively comforted her mother when she was seriously ill:

> She turns toward me, reaches out for me. "I'm scared. I'm scared" [she says]. I put my arms around her and hold her. I hold her as . . . she, once upon a time and long ago, held me. And I say the same words, the classic, maternal, instinctive words of reassurance. "Don't be afraid. I'm here. It's all right." . . . [But,] What's all right? What am I promising her? I'm scared, too. . . . How can I say it? But I do. I hold her close, kiss her, and murmur, "It's all right, Mother. It's all right." I mean these words. I don't understand them, but I mean them.

But sometimes we have to reach beyond human presence to discover the sustaining presence of God. Martin Luther King writes about his experience of walking through a dark and fearful valley where his only support came from the knowledge that Jesus was with him. He had launched a boycott of the segregated city bus system, and white opponents repeatedly threatened his life and the lives of his wife and baby daughter. One night a bomb was set off on his front porch. Several days later his phone rang at midnight, and the caller said, "Nigger, we are tired of you and your mess. And if you aren't out of town in three days, we're going to blow your brains out and blow up your house."

Years later, reflecting on that night, King related how he had sat at his kitchen table, on the verge of giving up. He recalls:

> With my cup of coffee sitting untouched before me I tried to think of a way to move out of the picture without appearing a coward. . . . I sat there and thought about a beautiful little daughter who had just been born. . . . She was the darling of my life. I'd come in night after night and see that little gentle smile. And I sat at that table thinking about that little girl and thinking about the fact that she could be taken away from me any minute. And I got to the point that I couldn't take it any longer. I was weak. Something said to me, you can't call on Daddy now; he's up in Atlanta, a hundred and seventy-five miles away. You can't even call on Mama now. You've got to call on that something in that person that your Daddy used to tell you about, that power that can make a way out of no way.
>
> And I discovered then that religion had to become real for me, and I had to know God for myself. And I bowed down over that cup of coffee. I'll never forget it. I prayed a prayer, and I prayed out loud that night. I said, "Lord, I'm down here trying to do what's right. But Lord, I must confess that I'm weak now. I'm faltering. I'm losing my courage."
>
> And it seemed at that moment that I could hear an inner voice saying to me, "Martin Luther, stand up for righteousness. Stand up for justice. Stand up for truth. And lo I will be with you, even until the end of the world." I heard the voice of Jesus saying still to fight on. He promised never to leave me, never to leave me alone. No never alone. No never alone. He promised never to leave me, never to leave me alone.

Ultimately, all fear is the fear of death. And the fears we experience along the journey of life are "little deaths" of greater or lesser proportions. So if we can gain the sense that there is nothing to fear in death, this will help us deal with the inevitable fears we face throughout our lives.

When I am preparing people for the funeral of a loved one, I often try to reassure them that death is not a lonely experience, but that God is with us in and through death. I read some verses from Psalm 139:

> Where can I go from your spirit?
> Or where can I flee from your presence?
> If I ascend to heaven, you are there;
> if I make my bed in Sheol [the grave], you are
>   there. . . .
> If I say, 'Surely the darkness shall cover me, and the
>   light around me be night',
> even the darkness is not dark to you;
> the night is as bright as day,
> for darkness is as light to you. (vv. 7–12)

A couple of years ago, Eugene O'Neill released a play on Broadway called *Lazarus Laughed*. Sadly it closed after only a week, but it actually had an intriguing storyline. The play begins with Lazarus (whom Jesus raised from the dead) emerging from the tomb. He'd been buried for four days when Jesus called him back to life. The first scene starts with Lazarus stumbling out of the darkness of the tomb, blinking under the bright sunlight. After he is helped out of the grave clothes he begins to laugh infectiously. He then hugs Jesus gratefully and is reunited with his two sisters.

Lazarus seems to be looking at the world differently, as if for the first time. He pats the earth, looks up to the blue sky, at the trees, at his neighbors, as if overwhelmed by the whole experience. Then he utters his first words: "Yes! Yes! Yes!"

Back at the house, where half the village has gathered, someone finally asks the question they all wanted to ask: "What is it like to die?" He says, "There is no death, really. There is only life. There is only God. There is only incredible joy. Death is not the way it appears from this side. Death is not an abyss into which we go into chaos. It is, rather, a portal through which we move into everlasting growth and everlasting life." He then says:

> The One that meets us there is the same generosity that gave us our lives in the beginning, the One who gave us our birth. Not because we deserved it but because that generous One wanted us to be and therefore there is nothing to fear in the next realm. The grave is as empty as a doorway is empty. It is a portal through which we move into greater and finer life. Therefore, there is nothing to fear. Our great agenda is to learn to accept, to learn to trust. We are put here to learn to love more fully. There is only life. There is no death.

And with that his laughter begins to fill the whole house.

We live in a terrifying world. But the only thing we truly need to know is that the generous God Lazarus speaks of in the play is with us; he surrounds us and always will surround us with his love.

When someone takes your hand in the dark, you're not afraid anymore. Darkness is frightening, but darkness and light are the same to God.

Relax. Breathe deeply. Repeat the words: "The Lord is my shepherd." And embrace the darkness as a friend who will help you grow.

Is there anybody there? I think you know the answer.

"Your rod and your staff—they comfort me"

LIFE IS DIFFICULT

"Life is difficult." This is how M. Scott Peck starts his massively successful book, *The Road Less Traveled*. The reason life is difficult, Peck tells us, is because life actually consists of a series of problems, and the process of confronting and solving problems is painful. We don't like that. Almost all of us, to a greater or lesser degree, try to avoid problems. We procrastinate, hoping that they will go away. We ignore them, forget them or pretend they don't exist.

Some of us even take drugs of one sort or another, to assist us in ignoring life's problems, so that by deadening ourselves to the pain we can forget the problems that caused the pain in the first place. We would rather skirt around the problems than face up to them. "We attempt to get out of them rather than suffer through them," as Peck puts it.

Some Christians follow the same strategy, using religion as a drug in order to ignore life's problems. Simplistic notions of an interventionist God who "won't let that happen to me" anesthetize them to the reality that bad things do happen to good people all the time—and that, one day, bad things will probably happen to them.

Psalm 23 has no sympathy with this approach to Christianity. There is no offer of a shortcut around the nasty bits in life. The assumption is that we will all face dark valleys and scary experiences at some stage.

The good news from both Scott Peck and the Bible is that difficulties, problems and pain will help us to grow as people, *once we learn how to deal with them.* Peck's approach to dealing with problems can be summarized in one word—discipline. "Discipline," he says, "is the basic set of tools we require to solve life's problems."

If you are anything like me—prone to being unfocused, undisciplined and disorganized—this may not come as particularly good news. Yet, in reality, very few things of any worth or substance are achieved in this world without discipline. This is equally true of religion as it is of relationships, sports, business, politics, art or music. The willingness to make personal sacrifices for the things we truly desire or believe in is fundamental to our success.

Drawing on the imagery of the ancient shepherd caring for his sheep, the twenty-third psalm focuses the issue more clearly. "Your rod and your staff—they comfort me." The rod and staff were the shepherd's everyday tools with which he would bring guidance, protection and discipline to the flock. Sometimes a wayward sheep would need to be firmly directed away from potential dangers, or one that had fallen into a ditch or a gully would need to be rescued. Sometimes threatening beasts would need to be confronted and driven away. The shepherd in this psalm is no pink fluffy figure who just lets the sheep ramble around at will. He recognizes the hazards and dangers out there and understands the need for tough love.

It is important to note that this statement, "Your rod and your staff—they comfort me," is directly linked to the experience of walking through the dark valley. Dark valleys are dangerous places, where faith is frequently ambushed, and perspective is easily lost. In these situations, life gets difficult, and a certain degree of discipline is essential if we are to survive.

In 2005 we witnessed a remarkable example of a family passing through the dark valley of pain and grief, following the racially aggravated murder of Anthony Walker, an eighteen-year-old black youth, who was also a devout Christian. Anthony was walking his girlfriend to a bus stop with his cousin in Huyton, Liverpool, when he was chased and murdered by two young white men, who were later convicted and jailed for life.

The level of media interest in this crime was understandable, but it was greatly compounded by the exceptional dignity and Christian testimony of Anthony's mother, Gee Walker, and other members of the family. After listening to every harrowing detail of the ambush that left her son with an ice axe embedded in his skull, Mrs. Walker spoke bravely of her ordeal, talking with compassion toward the two perpetrators.

Mrs. Walker was asked if she forgave the men. "I've got to forgive them," she replied. "My family stands by what we believe: forgiveness." Asked if Anthony's murder had tested her faith, she laughed as she said: "Lord, yes. My name's Gee, not Jesus! It's been hard, so hard, but I have to follow what the Lord teaches. It's easy to say those things, but when it is you who must do them, it is hard."

I found it interesting that when she was asked if she forgave the two men, Mrs. Walker hesitated for several seconds before replying. The pause was powerful and appropriate. Her forgiveness didn't come cheap. It was, as she said, something that her faith obliged her to do; it was an act of sacred discipline. I also noticed that she said her family placed the killers in God's hands.

I believe the Walker family teaches us a great deal about the interpretation of "Your rod and your staff—they comfort me," and about discipline as a redemptive tool when passing through dark valleys and frightening circumstances. Let me pinpoint three examples of what I mean.

The one thing it is difficult to maintain in a dark valley is *perspective*. The temptation is to succumb to self-pity and thereby lose the ability to see events in the context of a bigger picture. When we lose someone we love, when we experience a serious health scare, when we are betrayed or let down, when work disappears or finances run out, we all experience emotions such as sadness, grief, fear, jealousy and anger. The Walker family must have felt all of these in abundance, and much more. It is vital that we are allowed room to explore these feelings and work through them.

But self-pity does not work through feelings of grief, loss or anger; it clings to them, tenaciously. All perspective is lost. It is as though no one else is hurting, no one else suffers like this and no one understands. In this situation, the "comforting" discipline of the rod and staff are often far from welcome. The pain has now become a security blanket, and no one must take it away. But if we are to find a way through our dark valleys, it is essential to glimpse the bigger picture. We need to recognize that we are not alone in experiencing grief, loss and sadness, and that we live in a world heaving with pain and injustice. So while we weep our way through our own legitimate sorrows, we are redeemed from the destructive grip of self-pity.

Responsibility is a second redemptive discipline that helps us find a way through the dark valleys. Our natural instinct is to shift responsibility to others. I recently counseled a man who was not only lost in a dark valley, but who had dragged his entire family into the valley with him, through a serious problem of alcohol abuse. Yet, the one thing he would not do was take responsibility for his condition. The whole world was to blame: his wife, his kids, his boss, his parents, the government, the church.

Thankfully, I persuaded him to attend an Alcoholics Anonymous group where he discovered the Twelve Steps and learned the redemptive discipline of accepting personal responsibility.

In a quite different way, the Walker family demonstrated the meaning of accepting responsibility. Rather than reveling in self-pity, Mrs. Walker and her family took their destiny into their own hands by practicing *forgiveness*, which is also a redemptive discipline. It may seem strange to describe forgiveness as a discipline. We tend to think of forgiveness as something we feel, rather than as a discipline. But actually, the decision to forgive is just that—a decision. In the case of the Walker family it was a decision rooted in a deeply held Christian faith.

Forgiveness does not consist of a feeling, but the decision to forgive can seriously affect the way one feels. "Unforgiveness makes you a victim," Gee Walker told reporters, "and why should I be a victim? I have to practice what I preach. I don't feel any bitterness towards them really; truly, all I feel is . . . I feel sad for the family."

I once visited a woman in the hospital who had been ill for two or three years with various physical conditions. After a long chat, we arrived at the fact that she bore a searing resentment toward her father who had died some years before. She knew she needed to forgive him but felt that it was now too late, since he was deceased. I encouraged her to release her bitterness by verbally addressing her father and forgiving him. She thought this was silly, but agreed to do so. Tears rolled down her cheeks as she voiced her painful absolution to her dead father. Then, suddenly, she frantically grabbed the back of her neck and shouted out, "It's gone! It's gone!" Apparently she had felt a tight and painful knot in her neck for years, and now it had instantly departed. In a few days she returned home, fit and healthy, and virtually reborn. The redemptive discipline of forgiveness had brought "comfort" and led her through her long valley of darkness.

Life is difficult. What makes it difficult is the pain involved in dealing with problems. Problems such as the ones above create feelings of grief, loss, bitterness, resentment, sorrow, anger and frustration. "These are uncomfortable feelings," Scott Peck says, "often very uncomfortable, often as painful as any kind of physical pain, sometimes equaling the very worst kind of physical pain."

Anyone who suggests that life can be pain-free has not understood Psalm 23. Dark valleys are part of the human, spiritual journey. They cannot be avoided or sidestepped. However, the reassurance of the twenty-third psalm is that we need never face them alone. The shepherd-God is with us, offering relief and liberation through the power of redemptive discipline: "Your rod and your staff—they comfort me."

"You prepare a table before me in the presence of my enemies"

THE FEAST OF RECONCILIATION

Picture the scene: You are about to dine at one of the city's most celebrated restaurants. You are ushered to the plush lounge where you are served cocktails and have the chance to peruse the menu. After a short while the manager approaches to say that your table is ready, and he leads you through to the magnificent surroundings of the dining room. However, to your horror, as you approach the table you notice two very unwelcome guests waiting for you. The first is the conniving work colleague who wormed his way into the promotion that should have been yours; the other is that ghastly neighbor from hell who throws garbage into your garden and plays loud music when you are trying to get to sleep. You take a look at the table in dismay, realizing that in addition to your own place setting there are two others, one for each of them.

This is not dissimilar to the scene described in the twenty-third psalm, where it says: "You prepare a table before me in the presence of my enemies." It's a puzzling comment that is most commonly interpreted as saying, "You prepare a table for me, while my enemies are forced to look on." Phew, that's a relief! So those two wretched people in the restaurant are not actually sharing the meal with you on your big night out: they are being compelled to watch in mortified and mouth-watering silence while you are feasted like a lord.

It's an appealing thought: to be justified at the expense and to the humiliation of one's enemy. But it is also rather discomforting, especially in the context of a psalm that breathes tranquility and calm reassurance. As C. S. Lewis puts it in *Reflections on the Psalms*, it seems petty and vulgar that the writer's prosperity would not be complete unless "those horrid Joneses (who used to look down their noses at him) were watching it all and hating it." So, can this really be what the psalmist meant to convey?

Clearly, the Psalms are far from antiseptic where human emotion is concerned. Repeatedly, we find expressions of vengeance and violent retaliation along with passionate cries for divine retribution. So it may not seem unreasonable to recognize feelings of spite and vindictiveness, even in the shepherd psalm. If the Psalms teach us anything, it is the importance of honesty and authenticity. Too much religion is smothered with pious sentiment and moral pretense. Too many Christians say what they think they ought to say, or what they imagine other people want them to say, instead of what they truly feel. The Psalms, on the other hand, are gut-religion, voicing with devastating candor what the human heart actually feels.

There is an important lesson here. Burying feelings of anger, rage, resentment and frustration will prove bad for our physical and emotional health. They won't go away. They will fester and rankle beneath the surface, eventually being expressed in things like depression, despair, sourness and cynicism. The enjoyment of being vindicated while one's enemies are humiliated is hardly human experience at its most gracious and dignified, but in order to grow and move on, we must learn to own all our feelings for what they are, and then deal with them.

But in the light of the teachings and example of Jesus, we can also interpret this bit of Psalm 23 in a quite different way. Jesus teaches us to love our enemies, not to rub their noses in it when they are shown to be in the wrong. Just before he was arrested, Jesus shared a meal with those who misunderstood almost everything he was about; those who would betray and deny him, who would forsake him in his hour of greatest need. "Do good to those who hate you," he said, "bless those who curse you, pray for those who abuse you."

But who are one's enemies? What makes someone an enemy? According to the dictionary, an enemy is someone who hates and seeks to cause harm or cause trouble for somebody else. Sometimes it is easy to tell who one's enemies are. In the context of conventional war, for example, there can be little doubt who the enemy is. But in the world of global terrorism, we may have no idea who it is that means us harm. We may indeed share a table—or a seat on a bus or a subway—with someone who intends to blow us up, without having the faintest clue who they are.

But enemies are not simply those who threaten our physical well-being. To all intents and purposes, an enemy is someone whom we *feel* to be an enemy: someone who is a threat to our security, to our position or identity; someone whose influence we fear; someone who intimidates us with his or her talent or standing; someone whom we simply don't like, or who doesn't seem to like us.

Is it really possible to love such people, to love our enemies—real or imagined? Is it realistic to see oneself sitting at the same table as them, sharing a meal or a glass of wine? If it is, we will certainly need to discover new and different ways of looking at them, different ways of perceiving them. But how? How can such a change of outlook come about?

Richard Rohr suggests, in *Radical Grace*, that one vital key in learning to love our enemies is to understand that they may be telling us very important things about ourselves. Often, the things we reject and hate in others are in fact the things we dislike about ourselves. In the spiritual life our enemies may be our best friends, because they mirror aspects of ourselves that we need to face up to or deal with. It is in allowing the enemy at the gate to come in, allowing the "not-me" to enter our world, that we are able to face our own sin, our dark side.

Rohr isn't saying that we have to go out and become best friends with our enemies, but rather that we must wake up to the reality that our enemies are triggering something in us; that we need them. Until we learn to love the enemy within, we will struggle to love and forgive the "enemies" without.

Fear is another great barrier to being reconciled with one's enemies; and fear is perpetuated when, through ignorance and alienation, we treat them as faceless entities rather than see them as real people. There is a vast difference between looking people in the eye and talking about them behind their back. Looking them in the eye will probably enable us to recognize their vulnerability and anxiety; to appreciate that they have a partner and children; to realize that there may be reasons why they are so horrid. We may not like them any more for it, but we may feel more compassionate toward them. We may even pray for them. It is much harder to hate someone when you look him or her in the eye.

Sitting around a table sharing a meal demands eye contact. Unless we deliberately look down and leave the table as soon as possible, we are forced to acknowledge the other person. To eat together involves some level of intimacy. To pass the vegetables, to ask for the salt, to raise a glass and wish good health: these are things to do with friends and family, not with one's enemies. And in reality, most of us would avoid eating with an enemy, which may be why the psalm says, "*You* prepare a table in the presence of my enemies" (italics added). Things are different when we live in the presence of the great You, the shepherd-God who is never bound by human frameworks of enmity.

93

What happens when we sit around the table with our enemies? We eat and drink, speak and listen and share stories of happiness and pain. We discover other human beings. This is the radical, life-changing, all-transforming kingdom of God. How significant that the church finds its unique identity around a table, that a holy meal should be the cosmic symbol of healing and reconciliation. And how magnificent that the starter to this meal is the sharing of the peace. Never treat that sacred moment as a mere religious formality. The peace is the essential token of our willingness to be reconciled both with those we like and with those we dislike, with those with whom we agree and those with whom we disagree, with those who threaten us and with those to whom we are a threat. Unless we are ready to share the peace with all, we cannot in good faith participate in the mystery of Christ's love.

To eat, literally or metaphorically, with one's enemy is to share in the feast of divine reconciliation. It requires an attitude of forgiveness. And to forgive another person is, as Henri Nouwen says, an act of liberation. We set that person free from the negative bonds of enmity between us. We say, "I no longer consider you my enemy." But we also deliver ourselves from the burden of being the "offended one." "As long as we do not forgive those who have wounded us, we carry them with us or, worse, pull them as a heavy load." The deadly trap into which we so easily fall is that of propagating, maintaining and perpetuating a framework of enmity. Forgiveness liberates not only the other, but also one's self. It shatters the psychology of enmity and facilitates the re-imagining of relationship.

Gordon Wilson offered us one of the most stunning examples of reconciliation in recent times when he publicly forgave the IRA terrorists who had killed his daughter, Marie, along with nine other people in the Enniskillen bombing in 1987. He also begged that no one take revenge for Marie's death. "That will not bring her back," he said.

94

Gordon Wilson and his wife, Joan, were irreparably shattered by the loss of their daughter, but they desperately wanted to avoid an escalation of hatred and violence in Enniskillen, where Protestants and Catholics had lived peacefully side by side.

Throughout the rest of his life, Gordon Wilson worked tirelessly for reconciliation in Northern Ireland. The Irish government rewarded his work by making him a senator in the Irish parliament. He even came face to face with the people who had planned the Enniskillen bombing, asking them to stop the bombing and shooting. They refused, despite apologizing for killing Marie. After his death, many people in Northern Ireland carried on his work, and today the bombings and shootings have stopped in the province thanks to the healing work of people like Gordon Wilson, who dared to "dine" in the presence of his enemies.

The work of Desmond Tutu and the Commission for Truth and Reconciliation in South Africa offers another breathtaking example of the healing power of forgiveness. Tutu writes:

> We will look the beast in the eye. We will have come to terms with our horrendous past and it will no longer keep us hostage. We will cast off its shackles and, holding hands together, black and white will stride into the future, the glorious future God holds out before us—we who are the Rainbow people of God—and looking at our past we will commit ourselves to the future.

Tutu insists that negotiations take place not between friends but between enemies. And it is through such negotiations, through looking one's enemy in the eye, that enemies begin to find that they can actually become friends, or at least collaborators for the common good. But such negotiations, Tutu says, require risk-taking. They involve the willingness to compromise, to accommodate, and not to be intransigent, or to assert a bottom line.

Psalm 23 suggests that we will know that we have journeyed through the dark valley, that we have answered the threat of death, when we can sit at table with our enemy. The gospel of Christ fulfills the vision of the twenty-third psalm: "Then people will come from east and west, from north and south, and will eat in the kingdom of God."

The wisdom of the shepherd-God is seen not in outwitting one's enemies, not in crushing them or in humiliating them, but in befriending them. Abraham Lincoln was once asked why he tried to make friends with his enemies. "Surely, you should try to destroy them," the person said. Without a moment's hesitation, Lincoln gently replied, "Am I not destroying my enemies when I make them my friends?"

Desmond Tutu says that if we are to understand that God loves all of us, we must recognize that he loves our enemies too. "God does not share our hatred, no matter what the offense we have endured. We try to claim God for ourselves and for our cause, but God's love is too great to be confined to one side of a conflict or to any one religion."

This table is no human table. It is the table of the shepherd-God. It is a table of healing and forgiveness. It is the point of cosmic reconciliation. There are no sides here, no divisions and no exclusion. You are welcome. All are welcome.

"You anoint my head with oil; my cup overflows"

OVERWHELMING GRATITUDE

I have often been impressed by the way that some friends of ours gently deter people from referring to their three lovely children as "the triplets." Gabriel, Daisy and Millie are not simply part of some undistinguished "set," but individual people in their own right, and deserve to be treated as such.

The famous psychiatrist Elisabeth Kübler-Ross speaks of her struggle for identity, growing up as one of identical triplets. She even recalls sitting on her father's lap and being aware that he had no idea which of his daughters he was holding. The effect such an experience would have on one's sense of identity can only be imagined by most of us.

Human beings need to feel special, set apart from the crowd, unique. Even though, sometimes, we may be happy to merge with the crowd, we still need to feel special, to be special to someone. It is an appetite that caters to a basic human requirement, which is different from, but equally important to, food and drink. Feeling special nourishes the soul and nurtures a sense of well-being.

Knowing that we are identified as individuals before God is an essential element in both Judaism and Christianity, despite the deeply communal nature of each faith.

Psalm 23 begins, "The Lord is *my* shepherd," and not, "The Lord is *our* shepherd" (italics added). Elsewhere in the Psalms, David talks about God forming him in his mother's womb and being acquainted with all his idiosyncrasies (Ps. 139:1–18).

No doubt drawing on the imagery of the twenty-third psalm, Jesus describes himself as the Good Shepherd who *calls his own sheep by name* (John 10:3, italics added). Being named is an important part of feeling special. We all love it when someone unexpectedly remembers our name. Much more than this is implied, however, in the statement that the Good Shepherd calls his own sheep by name. This is not simply an accurate roll call, but an indication that we are all fully known and fully loved by the shepherd of our souls.

In Psalm 23, the writer's uniqueness before God is celebrated with the exclamation: "You anoint my head with oil." While it is commonly assumed that David wrote these words, the anointing referred to here is not the royal anointing that he received as king, but an anointing of joy and blessing. David knew he was beloved of God (which is what his name means) regardless of whether or not he became king.

Traditionally, Christians are anointed at baptism. And in the case of children this is generally associated with naming. The alternative term "christening" (derived from "Christ," the "anointed one") brings together the actions of naming and anointing in the context of the child being welcomed into the family of the church and affirmed in his or her uniqueness before God.

I have never lost the sense of awe I first felt when a child was handed to me for baptism. Each and every time I pour holy water on a baby and smear the oil of chrism on a tiny forehead, I wonder whom this scrap of flesh and blood will become, whom they will love, where they will go, what they will do with their particular gift of life. Most of all, I marvel afresh that, out of the countless billions who have ever walked the earth, God recognizes and embraces this child.

There are in fact many occasions when anointing with oil might be administered in the church: during services of confirmation or ordination, for healing or as part of some other special act of blessing.

In recent years it has been our practice at St. Luke's to celebrate the baptism of Jesus, on the second Sunday in Epiphany, with a service of public anointing. I know of few things more moving than the sight of people holding out their hands to receive the oily mark of the cross on their upturned palms. Just as Jesus set out on his public ministry with the voice of God ringing in his ears—"You are my Son, the Beloved, with whom I am well pleased" (Matt. 3:17)—so we, who go out to serve God in our world in our own particular ways, also need to know that we are beloved of God.

The words "my cup overflows" are a proclamation of delight and gratitude. The psalmist knows his deepest wants will be satisfied. He has discovered tranquility of spirit and found food for the soul. His path, though sometimes dark and scary, has never been solitary. And now, seated at the table prepared for him, and anointed with the oil of God's blessing, his heart is ready to burst. Thankfulness wells up within him. His cup is full to the brim and runs over.

Friedrich Schleiermacher, the nineteenth-century German theologian, said that religion is the external expression of internal feelings of faith. Of all the internal religious feelings, none is more fundamental than gratitude. Gratitude is the consummate religious expression. Even when it is not acknowledged as a religious impulse, gratitude draws the human heart God-ward. People of all faiths and no faith constantly feel thankful for the gifts they enjoy—fresh air, warm sunshine and refreshing rain, friends and family, food and drink, beauty and imagination, the exhilaration of a job well done and the gift of life itself. A million things evoke gratitude toward someone or something beyond ourselves—whether or not we feel able to define who or what that someone or something is.

Gratitude shapes who we are as people. It creates humility and generosity; it undermines pretentiousness and self-interest. Grateful people make the most of living today. They don't postpone life until they succeed, until they are financially secure, until they are married or their children are grown up or until they win the lottery or retire. Grateful people live now, with the liberating realization that now is all they have. The opening lines of Morning Prayer in *Common Worship* say:

> As we rejoice in the gift of this new day,
> so may the light of your presence, O God,
> set our hearts on fire with love for you;
> now and forever. Amen.

But can we feel grateful all of the time, for all the things that happen in our lives? The temptation is to divide life up between the good things that we enjoy or look forward to, and for which we feel grateful, and the bad things that we endure, gritting our teeth and choosing quickly to forget. Forgetting the negative things, however, is seldom as easy as it seems. Regrets have a habit of lurking in the back of the mind, coloring our vision of the present and inhibiting our approach to the future.

"True spiritual gratitude," Henri Nouwen suggests, "embraces all of our past, the good as well as the bad events, the joyful as well as the sorrowful moments." I confess I haven't always found this easy to put into practice. Sometimes I have found myself wishing away bits of my past. Being so happy with where I am and who I am now, I wish I had been here all along; I wish I could claw back some of the years I regret. However, my wife, who is far wiser than

I am, reassures me that I am only who I am today because of who I was yesterday; that I could not have gotten where I am now without being there first. This does not mean, of course, that all that happened in the past was good, but it does mean that it is part of who I am as a person. And by embracing the whole of it, by recognizing God's loving presence even in the parts I wish hadn't happened, the past becomes redeemed.

Most of us have things in our lives that we find it difficult to be grateful for; things we feel guilty or embarrassed about, things we would wish to alter, things that were forced upon us by others. But once we have the courage to embrace the whole of who we are, the past, like the present, can be converted into a means of divine grace.

Such transformations do not occur overnight. Real gratitude cannot be forced. Psalm 23 teaches that life is a journey; and on that journey we sometimes feel calm and contented, sometimes frightened, sometimes surrounded by darkness and sometimes confronted by enemies. Eventually we feel overwhelmed by God's goodness as we see hope and expectation rise from the ashes of regret and despair. But the stages of this journey cannot be rushed. We must allow ourselves time to feel sad, disappointed, angry or bereaved, knowing that the promise of the psalm is that such feelings will pass, given time. Eventually, we will find the wherewithal to be grateful for the whole of life.

From a Christian perspective, it is inevitable that the words "my cup overflows" will take our minds to the Eucharist. *Eucharist* means "thanksgiving." How wonderful that the central ritual of Christian faith and worship is a celebration of gratitude. Each time the chalice is raised to our lips, we are reminded of the vast debt of gratitude we owe to God and to all who have loved us and sacrificed on our behalf. The cup of blessing is filled to the brim and running over. We give thanks for the generosity of a redeeming God and the world he created.

What are we to do with this cup of blessing but drink from it deeply? The best thing we can do with a gift is use it. Our bodies are gifts to be cared for and placed in the service of others. Our minds are gifts to be exercised and stretched with new thoughts and ideas. Our imagination is a gift to challenge accepted conventions and humdrum assumptions. Our senses are gifts to be nourished with sights and sounds and feelings of beauty. Food, drink, laughter and fun are gifts to share often with friends, loved ones and strangers. We express gratitude by putting to good use the gifts with which we are blessed. G. K. Chesterton, when he wrote his autobiography close to the end of a long and rich life, tried to define in a sentence the most important lesson he had learned. He concluded that the vital thing was whether one took things for granted or took them with gratitude.

There is a Jewish saying that we will have to give account on the judgment day of every good thing that we refused to enjoy when we might have done so.

God our life, be with us through this day, whether or not it brings us joy. Help us when evening comes to recall one benefit, for which to give you thanks. Amen.

A New Zealand Prayer Book

"Surely goodness and mercy shall follow me all the days of my life"

GRACE—THE HOUND OF HEAVEN

In the winter of 1887, the editor of a Catholic literary review called *Merry England* received a package of essays and poems with a cover letter that read:

> Dear Sir,
>
> In enclosing the accompanying article for your inspection, I must ask pardon for the soiled state of the manuscript. It is due, not to slovenliness, but to the strange places and circumstances under which it has been written . . . I enclose a stamped envelope for a reply . . . I shall regard your judgment of its worthlessness as quite final . . . Apologizing very sincerely for my intrusion on your valuable time,
>
> I remain,
> Yours with little hope,
> Francis Thompson
> P.S. Kindly address your rejection to the Charing Cross Post Office.

After a cursory glance at the package, the editor tossed it onto a shelf, where it remained for several months.

Francis Thompson hailed from a good Catholic family. His father was a doctor and wanted his son also to study medicine, even though his real passion was poetry. After a massive row with his father and the sudden death of his mother, Thompson's world crumbled. He flunked his exams and took to the streets, where he became an opium addict. And it was out there, living as a tramp in a drug-induced haze, that Thompson wrote the poetry he sent to the magazine.

Once the editor read the manuscripts properly, he quickly recognized the mark of a genius. He wanted to meet Thompson, but had no idea how to track him down since Charing Cross Post Office knew nothing of his whereabouts. So he published some of the poems in the hope that Thompson would read them and make himself known. Sure enough, the bedraggled man turned up at the magazine's offices, overjoyed at the recognition of his work. He was immediately dispatched to a clinic to dry out, and then to a monastery to convalesce.

During those months of retreat, Francis Thompson penned his most famous poem, "The Hound of Heaven," which was inspired by the line in the twenty-third psalm: "Surely goodness and mercy shall follow me all the days of my life." Through all the destitution, despair and drug addiction he was unable to outrun those "strong feet" that followed him with "unhurrying chase and unperturbed pace." For Francis Thompson, God's love was like a great hound that would never cease pursuing him.

The prospect of being chased by a hound, albeit a heavenly hound, may sound pretty scary. Yet it is an image that is entirely consistent with the phrasing of Psalm 23 that says, "goodness and mercy shall *follow* me . . ." (italics added). The thought is in fact much stronger in the original Hebrew, which suggests that goodness and mercy shall *pursue* me—chase me down wherever I go.

There is an obvious connection here with the parable of the lost sheep, where Jesus says that the owner will track down the sheep until he finds it. The sense is of a shepherd who has no intention whatsoever of giving up until he recovers that sheep. The outcome of the story is clear: the shepherd-God will never abandon us, however wayward we may be.

Jesus doesn't stop there: he tells two more stories that make the same point in different ways. The first is of a woman who loses a silver coin and searches tirelessly until she finds it; the other is about a loving father who yearns for the return of his wayward son.

Some commentators view the parable of the prodigal son as an exposition of Psalm 23. More specifically, it can be viewed as an elucidation of this one line: "Surely goodness and mercy shall follow me all the days of my life." Even though the father in the parable does not literally pursue his son, badgering and pestering him to return home, it is clear that the young man is hounded by the goodness and grace of his father.

"Surely goodness and mercy shall follow me." The word *mercy* is a translation of the Hebrew word *hesed*, more commonly translated as "loving-kindness." Books have been written about this one word, which is best thought of as unconditional or unearned love—what Christians talk about as "grace." "Surely goodness and mercy shall follow me" is all about grace—that special word we use to encapsulate the quality of divine love, love that is entirely unmerited and undeserved, and that knows no limit.

Francis Thompson hits the nail on the head when he says in his poem that human love "needs human meriting." But God's love has nothing to do with merit. There is nothing that any of us can do or say that will cause God to love us any more or less. Nothing about us surprises or shocks God. Nothing makes him tired or weary of loving us. When we have a bad day, God still loves us. When we screw up a relationship, God still loves us. When we choose a wrong turn, God still loves us. When we cannot muster the faith to believe he exists, God still loves us. When we live selfishly, when we behave like a spoiled child, when we make a complete twit of ourselves—God still loves us

. . . the hound of heaven pounds on after us. In a nutshell, the twenty-third psalm has one uncomplicated message: we are loved simply because we are.

Einstein asked the question, Is the universe a friendly place? Psalm 23 offers an ambiguous reply: the world contains many unfriendly elements that threaten to engulf us, but in and through and above all other things the universe is permeated with a loving presence that pursues us constantly and seeks to do us good. "Surely goodness and mercy shall follow me all the days of my life."

That said, undoubtedly there are things in life that do need to be earned or merited. And it is important that this is so: the human psyche thrives on challenges. Almost invariably, we achieve more when more is expected of us. Football players must merit a place on the field; couples have to work hard to maintain strong, healthy relationships; and students need to study arduously to obtain good results. Yet the most fundamental thing that every man, woman and child needs to understand is that they are loved for no other reason than that they are. I may not make the starting lineup on the team; my marriage or partnership may flounder; I may flunk all my exams, but the one thing I should know is that I am accepted—come what may.

Some people will become jittery at this point, worrying that I am dishing up "cheap" grace. But that is the whole point about grace: it's not only cheap—it's free! You can't buy it for love or money; it's a gift. God does not say, "Do what I want you to, and then I'll love you."

He says, "Please listen: if you keep on traveling down that road, you are going to get hurt. But know this: I will still pursue you. I will always be with you. And I will never, never stop loving you." You can't outrun the hound of heaven: *surely* goodness and mercy will follow you all the days of your life.

Several years ago, the American journalist Bill Moyers made a documentary called *Amazing Grace* in which he traveled around the world interviewing all kinds of people whose lives had been touched or changed by John Newton's dearly loved hymn. He asked each of them which was their favorite part of the song. Without hesitation, people like Johnny Cash pointed straight to the third verse:

> Through many dangers, toils and snares,
> I have already come;
> 'tis grace hath brought me safe thus far,
> and grace will lead me home.

Judy Collins, the folk singer, talked about her struggles with drugs and alcoholism. When she saw no way out it was singing "'tis grace hath brought me safe thus far, and grace will lead me home" that brought her back from the edge and healed her troubled mind. Moyers even went behind the bars of Folsom Prison in Texas and talked with prisoners, some on death row. One by one they said that it was the third verse that always got to them the most; it is the verse that points to the dogged, tireless grace of God—the hound of heaven that never gives up the chase.

The point at which many people's lives have been transformed is when they stop running away from love and embrace it. This may not be a specifically religious experience. The hound of heaven runs down many roads; God's grace is manifest in a million different ways. Last week I officiated at the funeral of a man named Ted. Before the funeral I struggled to discover anything about this man. I spoke to his brother, who told me that he liked to keep fit and loved chocolate mousse—that's it! He couldn't even tell me the name of his brother's deceased wife. As I waited for Ted's remains to arrive at the crematorium, I felt overwhelmingly sad that eighty-three years on this earth would end at a funeral attended by two relatives who had never visited him during his final years in the nursing home, and a vicar who had nothing personal to say about him.

Then I noticed the lone figure of a woman standing outside the crematorium. I approached her and asked if she knew Ted. She said that she was the manager of the home where he'd spent the last ten years of his life. I shook her hand warmly and said how pleased I was that she was there. In the few moments before the hearse arrived she smiled broadly as she told me one story after another about Ted and the fun her staff had with him. That conversation changed everything. Now I had too much to say about Ted, who was no longer merely a "deceased," but a person. Five minutes earlier, I had found myself questioning how much goodness and mercy had followed Ted through his final years, but now I realized that he had indeed been loved simply for who he was. Doctrines, theology, God-words and religious trappings are not necessary in order for God to be present.

Frederick Buechner, in *Listening to Your Life*, says the following about the unconditional grace and goodness of God:

> The grace of God means something like: Here is your life. You might never have been, but you are because the party wouldn't have been complete without you. Here is the world. Beautiful and terrible things will happen. Don't be afraid. I am with you. Nothing can separate us. It's for you that I created the universe. I love you.

"I will dwell in the house of the Lord forever"

HOME IS WHERE THE HEART IS

Like every good story, Psalm 23 has a beginning, a middle and an end. It starts with the writer affirming his faith in the shepherd-God who watches over his flock, providing for their every need and leading them to rich pastures beside calm clear waters.

The middle part of the story is quite different. The mood changes, the setting switches from tranquil lakes and fields to a dark valley signifying pain, loss and adversity. The pathway is rough and uneven, and it's difficult to see the way forward. Yet the message is clear: even in our darkest nights, amid feelings of fear and despair, we are never alone. The road may indeed be dark and frightening, but the shepherd-God is close at hand, bringing support and reassurance that all will be well.

Then, as the story moves to a conclusion, the mood changes again. Gone is the darkness and gloom, replaced by a renewed sense of ease and belonging. And now there is a strong awareness that the sunshine after the darkness is much sweeter than the sunshine experienced before the passage through the dark valley. Far from destroying us, difficulties and setbacks can cause us to grow as people and mature in our faith. Only through doubts and questions can that faith develop beyond shallow certainties and assumptions into a deep and mellow trust in God.

The psalm closes with the assuring realization that nothing will ever truly separate us from God's loving presence: "I will dwell in the house of the LORD forever." This, like the psalm as a whole, can sound like soppy religious sentiment. Yet nothing could be further from the truth. In this psalm the writer distills a mature reflection on the sum total of life: the realization that true joy and meaning come from loving God and being loved by God. A warm presence dwells at the heart of the universe, a God who desires to commune with human beings forever.

There is, of course, a future dimension to dwelling in the house of the Lord. Some versions of the Bible have "forever" (KJV), while others render it "my whole life long" (NRSV). The truth is, the verse implies both meanings.

It is the "forever," the life hereafter bit, that tends to cause most problems for those on the edges or on the outside of faith. Karl Marx argued that religion is the opiate of the people—pie in the sky when you die that keeps you from asking too many questions about the here and now. Marx had a point: by telling us to concentrate on the hereafter rather than on the here and now, the church has often, inadvertently, colluded with the political status quo. While people hanker after their sweet post-mortem pie, they turn their backs on the task of transforming the world in the present.

This approach to Christianity is not uncommon. The present world is frequently portrayed as "enemy" territory, ruled by forces of darkness and beyond redemption. Accordingly, there is no use trying to improve things because they cannot be improved—the world has had it; we must now set our sights on heaven.

I personally grew up with this kind of Christianity. It was succinctly summed up in the words of a popular song at the time, in which the singer said that the world was not

115

his home—he was simply passing through to something and somewhere better.

Pie in the sky Christianity can be thought of like this: imagine the world as a kind of cosmic hotel, a stopping-off place on the long and winding road to heaven. The hotel is still seen as a place of beauty. After all, God did originally create it, and it continues to bear the marks of this in its design and construction, especially in its lush surrounding gardens—the countryside. But the devil has managed to get in and somehow take possession of the place. It is now filthy and rat infested. As a result, the future of the hotel is limited: soon it will be completely destroyed. But before God's demolition mob gets to work, a bus will turn up to carry away God's faithful people to their heavenly home far down the road. Meanwhile they are warned not to unpack their bags or get attached to their rooms, or worse still, enjoy the leisure facilities too much. Their job is to warn the other guests of the hotel's impending doom and to be prepared for a hasty getaway once the heavenly bus arrives.

Is this what the psalm means when it speaks of dwelling in God's house forever—pie in the sky when you die? Definitely not. I like Archbishop Desmond Tutu's comment when he says that a church that tells us not to concentrate on the things of this world but simply on the things of the next world needs to be treated with "withering scorn and contempt as being not only wholly irrelevant but actually blasphemous." Strong words, but Archbishop Tutu has seen too much of the complacency bred by this kind of Christianity: complacency about solving problems like poverty, hunger and HIV/AIDS, or fighting prejudice and social and political injustice; the complacency that reduces Christian mission to saving souls instead of redeeming people.

The Book of Psalms utterly refutes pie in the sky religion. Again and again, the Psalms call for justice, for the lifting of oppression, for an end to hunger and poverty—not in the next world but in this present world, here and now.

That said, there is, of course, a future dimension to dwelling in the house of the Lord. Some versions of the Bible translate verse 6 as saying, "I will dwell in your house forever"; others render it, "I will dwell in your house for the rest of my days." The truth is, the verse implies both meanings. Traditional Christian teaching certainly affirms both an earthly and a heavenly interpretation of what it means to dwell in the house of the Lord. The Christian hope encompasses both the present and the future, the "already" and the "not yet."

Desmond Tutu's hope for South Africa was always that the future would break into the present; that heaven would penetrate hellish earthly reality. In his wonderfully inspiring book, *God Has a Dream*, Tutu argues that this is precisely what did happen in South Africa with the collapse of apartheid. Some of the glorious liberty of God's eternal house invaded the oppression and injustice of South African society and politics, opening up a whole new era, an era that few expected to see in their lifetime. This doesn't mean, of course, that everything is now perfect in South Africa. But there are now glimpses of God's kingdom in that magnificent country, as centuries of structural and cultural racism and demonic injustice have come tumbling down, and a process of truth and reconciliation is under way.

The reality is, God's house is a very spacious place—maybe too spacious for most of us to cope with. Arguably the most challenging chapter in Desmond Tutu's book is entitled "God Loves Your Enemies." Without in any way covering up the horror of the atrocities committed against black people in South Africa, the archbishop makes it quite clear that there is no way that his country could move on without a willingness—and a process—for reconciliation between oppressor and oppressed. Nothing symbolizes this better than his account of how Nelson Mandela invited his former jailer to be a VIP guest at his inauguration. Anger

117

and hatred must be replaced with forgiveness. Clearly, Mandela's vision of God's place is pretty spacious.

But we all need spaciousness and a place for our hearts to belong. The Western world in particular is experiencing a crisis of belonging. We yearn for a place to be, a home for the heart. Psalm 23 offers the prospect of such a home: dwelling in the house of God. Yet sadly, in our search for such a place, we often end up with an illusion of belonging, a false sense of home.

In a consumerist world, we are offered a stake in community: buying into a feeling of being "in," of being "cool," of being "where it's at." But it is an illusion, a marketing ploy that feeds off our existential loneliness and the misapprehension that social conformity equals social acceptance or somewhere to belong. In reality, many are simply left with the "fellowship" of material possessions and a credit card bill that has to be paid. And it's not just the "haves" who become victims to the false promise of a consumerist community. The "have nots" are caught in the same delusion, sensing that the absence of the latest accessories to a successful life means that they are excluded and don't really belong.

Home is an evocative word, signifying many different things, and not all positive. Some people leave home as soon as possible, finding it too narrow, too stifling. For some, home is a place of abuse or violence. But for most people, home signifies things like security, safety, familiarity, comfort and, most of all, acceptance.

People who travel a lot know very particularly how precious the feeling of home can be. For many years, travel was a major part of my own work and ministry. It was not unusual to find myself in Africa or South America or elsewhere for three or four weeks at a time. I loved the work, and I enjoyed meeting new people and visiting new places, but I found it hard to be away from home. I once spent five weeks journeying around Argentina, speaking night after night to large and small church communities in chapels and halls and under trees. I was so homesick by the end of it that I cried myself to sleep one night.

What was it that I missed most? My wife and the children, of course. But in particular I missed the sense of unconditional love and acceptance that home symbolizes, knowing that I was accepted without reserve. I knew that when I returned, it wouldn't matter if I had failed miserably in my mission, if people had hated my talks or disagreed profoundly with what I had to say. I would just be accepted; I would belong—come what may.

This is about as close as I can get in describing what the notion of dwelling in God's house means to me. It's to know that whatever goes wrong, that however much I might screw up, God's arms of love are held out to me. In an angst-ridden world, Psalm 23 stands as a beacon of hope, the promise of somewhere to belong, somewhere to be, which is safe, warm and welcoming.

From a Christian perspective, the church is the most powerful symbol of the house of the Lord—or it should be. John O'Donohue, in *Eternal Echoes*, certainly questions whether the institutions of the church provide a place to belong. "The institutions of religion have really diminished," he says, "and fallen into the hands of frightened functionaries who are great custodians of the gateways but don't really know what the landscapes are like further in towards the heart of the mystery."

It is very difficult for institutions to remain hospitable; by nature they do indeed become the haunt of "frightened functionaries." The sense of being a spiritual home is much more likely to be found in a local expression of church. I hope that is how you experience your church: as a place to be, a place of inclusivity, a place where nothing has to be proved, a place of acceptance, a place to belong, a home for the heart.

Jesus says, "In my Father's house are many dwelling places." This gives me the picture of a massive rambling mansion where everyone has his or her own space, but where there are also spacious rooms to gather with friends for fun and fellowship.

The message of Psalm 23 is God saying, "Come over to my place. Move in. Make yourself at home. Find some space. But mix in with everybody too. You've arrived. You're known. There's nothing to say, nothing to prove . . . you're part of the family. You're welcome. You're home."

NOTES

1. Mary Schertz from an article entitled "Sheepish" in *The Christian Century*, April 20, 2004, 17.

2. Harold Kushner from an Internet interview with "Religion & Ethics Newsletter" at http://www.pbs.org/wnet/religionandethics/week813/feature.html.

References

Barnes, Craig, *Searching for Home: Spirituality for Restless Souls*. Grand Rapids: Brazos Press, 2003.

The Book of Psalms with an Introduction by Bono. The Pocket Canons. Edinburgh: Canongate Books, 1999.

Brueggemann, Walter, *The Message of the Psalms*. Minneapolis: Augsburg, 1984.

Brueggemann, Walter, *The Threat of Life: Sermons on Pain, Power and Weakness*. Minneapolis: Fortress Press, 1996.

Buechner, Frederick, *The Clown in the Belfry*. San Francisco: HarperCollins, 1992.

Buechner, Frederick, *Listening to Your Life: Daily Meditations*. San Francisco: HarperCollins, 1992.

Carson, Clayborne, ed., *The Autobiography of Martin Luther King*. London: Abacus, 2000.

Hornok, Marcia K., "Psalm 23." *Discipleship Journal*, 60 (1990).

Japanese Psalm 23, quoted in June Cotner, *Bless the Day: Prayers and Poems to Nurture Your Soul*. New York: Kodansha America Inc., 1998.

Kübler-Ross, Elisabeth, *On Children and Death*. New York: Macmillan, 1983.

Kushner, Harold, *The Lord Is My Shepherd: The Healing Wisdom of the Twenty-third Psalm*. London: Hodder & Stoughton, 2003.

Lasn, Kalle, *Culture Jam: The Uncooling of America*. New York: Eagle Brook, 1999.

L'Engle, Madeleine, *Glimpses of Grace*. New York: Harper-Collins, 1998.

Lewis, C. S., *A Grief Observed*. London: Faber and Faber, 1961.

Lewis, C. S., *Reflections on the Psalms*. London: Geoffrey Bles, 1958.

Merton, Thomas, *Conjectures of a Guilty Bystander*. New York: Doubleday, 1989.

Moore, Thomas, *Care of the Soul*. London: Piatkus Books, 1992.

Nervo, Amado, Prayer quoted on The Spirituality Book Club website: http://www.spiritualbookclub.com/prayer.

A New Zealand Prayer Book. San Francisco: HarperCollins, 1997.

Nouwen, Henri, *Bread for the Journey: Reflections for Every Day of the Year*. London: Darton, Longman and Todd, 1996.

O'Donohue, John, *Eternal Echoes: Exploring Our Hunger to Belong*. London: Bantam Books, 1998.

O'Neill, Eugene, "Lazarus Laughed." *Complete Plays 1920–1931*. New York: Library of America, 1988.

Peck, M. Scott, *The Road Less Traveled*. London: Rider, 1978.

Rohr, Richard, *Radical Grace*. Cincinnati: St. Anthony Messenger Press, 1995.

Seuss, Dr., *Oh, the Places You'll Go!* London: HarperCollins, 1990.

Tillich, Paul, *Shaking the Foundations*. Harmondsworth: Penguin, 1949.

Tutu, Desmond, *God Has a Dream*. London: Rider, 2004.

Yaconelli, Mike, *Messy Spirituality: Christianity for the Rest of Us*. London: Hodder & Stoughton, 2001.

Dave Tomlinson is vicar of St. Luke's Church, Holloway, North London. He set up, and for ten years led, Holy Joes, an unconventional church group meeting in a London pub. He holds a master's degree in biblical interpretation and is author of the bestselling book *Post-Evangelical* (Triangle, 1995) and *Running into God* (SPCK, 2004). He is married with three children and three grandchildren.